Green Branding

Oliver Errichiello • Arnd Zschiesche

Green Branding

Basics, Success Factors And Instruments
For Sustainable Brand And Innovation
Management

 Springer

Oliver Errichiello
Office for Brand Development
Hamburg, Germany

Arnd Zschiesche
Office for Brand Development
Hamburg, Germany

ISBN 978-3-658-36059-7   ISBN 978-3-658-36060-3   (eBook)
https://doi.org/10.1007/978-3-658-36060-3

This Springer imprint is published by the registered company Springer Fachmedien Wiesbaden GmbH part of Springer Nature.
The registered company address is: Abraham-Lincoln-Str. 46, 65189 Wiesbaden, Germany

"It would be a comfort to our feeble souls and our works if all things were to pass away as slowly as they come into being; but as it is, growth proceeds slowly, while the road to ruin is swift."
Lucius Annaeus Seneca (91st letter to his friend Lucilius)
For Morten Jacob and Bent Jonathan
O.E.
For Leander, Leonas, and Xena
A.Z.

Preface

Since 2016, the first edition of *Green Brand Management* has enjoyed an extremely resonant response in Germany, Austria, and Switzerland. We would like to thank entrepreneurs, scientists, and students for their valuable support. Furthermore, social developments and new political frameworks made it seem sensible to edit the first edition again thoroughly. The result is the updated and critically revised edition of *Green Brand Management* and the first translation in English.

"Green business" remains an exciting topic and a difficult challenge: On the carpet floors of this world, the question has been asked for some time: What is actually our "purpose"? Sufficient studies have clearly shown that companies gain economic advantages from setting "higher" goals than just economic success. The pursuit of profit, sustainability, and social commitment must be combined for the sake of profit. If you save the planet and society convincingly enough and put ethics first, you get public goodwill ... and at the end of the day, maybe a tiny bit of money for it. The things you don't do to escape the mundane stigma of sales.

And then corona also hit the planet. The competition for the "Most Good" company was on. Who is the *most purposeful organisation on our planet?* All the many commercials from the big brands during that time wished us "good health", motivated us to "stay at home", or simply painted an emotional morality tale of the lovably chaotic daily life of the home office: The Family is the Last Remaining Adventure of Modernity ... Companies understood us and our everyday lives; they were emotionally close to us.

All this is subsumed under "purpose", i.e. a truly relevant (higher) purpose that a brand should contain nowadays if it wants to be relevant to the public at all. Behind this is a zeitgeisty conviction: The performance of a company itself is deeply interchangeable and therefore not newsworthy. Only "added value" can save us. Purpose means exclusively an ethical purposefulness. The deeply serious person of hyper-modernity wants to link even the consumption of a turnip with meaningfulness. The focus is not on satiety, but above all on the very good feeling of thinking and doing something exceedingly right. After all, every purchase decision illustrates how we see ourselves and want to be seen. And we are better, much better than everyone before. So the "good feeling" acts as a key to people's hearts and, virtually incidentally, to their wallets. What seems droll has grown over the years into an ever more comprehensive claim: today, products and services have to save the whole world.

The fact that everyone is stirring the identical emotional creative solution seems beside the point. The main thing is short: violent effects that don't necessarily have to be reflected in the box office. "It's only image advertising" is the accepted excuse. Let's be honest: Have you permanently linked a single one of the emotional spots of the last few years with a brand? Probably not. Because when it really matters, when it really becomes relevant, it's always the concrete performance alone that counts, not the feeling.

If we are really honest, then the advertising-business grab for the good is all the more vicious: Purpose campaigns have the effect of quickly and strikingly creating the impression of "activity" and are much cheaper than a fundamental strategic adjustment of the business model towards more justice, fairness, or sustainability. They remain on the surface, so they fit the zeitgeist perfectly.

True public spirit is when customers, suppliers, and raw material producers at all levels receive adequate value for their services and together try to find better solutions for people, animals, and the environment in their daily business. But all this is based on real work and not on "green show".

It remains the case that the decisive and sole purpose of a serious company is to maintain the trust of its customers and the wider public in its own services—primarily through really good services, not through communication. This demonstrates public spirit, because the steady cycle of money in exchange for trust in the quality of products ensures that the entrepreneur can pay his employees and convince people of a meaningful economy, get them excited about it, and make contributions to the common good—not just in the form of taxes. That is farsighted public and environmental sense.

Hamburg, Germany   Oliver Errichiello
October 2021   Arnd Zschiesche

What Is This Book About?

This book is about services that strengthen people and nature. The decisive tool for clearly strengthening these services in competition is neither one's own bad conscience nor an ethical drive: it is the brand. The brand? Aren't we used to brands being evil, seducing, and manipulating us? Distracting people from their true purpose and desires? Brand excites people about things they don't need at all—for the sole purpose of maximising profits. That's a common blanket accusation.

Isn't it a social drama, optionally also an educator trauma, that children already know the logos of multinational corporations, but can't distinguish an oak leaf from a maple leaf? That social acceptance in the classroom in some places depends on the symbol on their sneakers or T-shirt? Even more alarming: many adults (still) seem to define themselves by signs and lettering on their wristwatches, handbags, and car bonnets—the "new luxury" or not—the luxury industry is doing better than ever. What's more, especially among "social high achievers" in the usual industries, it is not primarily green products that are used to underpin one's status. Rather, it's rolling, resource-guzzling luxury tanks with 500 hp and fuel consumption approaching that of helicopters. So what does one have to do with the other?

From a brand sociological, i.e. strictly structural, point of view, it makes no difference whatsoever whether we are talking about Porsche, Shell, McDonald's or Greenpeace, Alnatura, and the Armedangels. All of these enterprises interpret and shape the world in their very own way—thereby attracting certain people and repelling others, often for exactly the same reasons. Spontaneous sayings like "I'd never sit in that" or "Only eco-wackos eat that" are brute condensations of long-standing experiential values that we don't even have to have experienced ourselves. Brands are performance bodies around which people gather because they find this one specific performance attractive and because such brand bodies act predictably. They thus structure the complex world and simplify it for us at one point in our daily lives. Strong brands possess social magnetism—some of them can magically attract us; others can be chosen by us as an enemy image. In both cases, social energy is activated in us: "typical BMW driver" or "brilliant car, great guy". We consume most brand services on a daily basis almost unconsciously; their purchase has become a good habit that we no longer (want to) think about. The human tendency to habituation and habit is an economic blessing for brands—and reason for existence. The equally human tendency to draw boundaries with others—consciously or unconsciously—another. In short, brand is deeply human from every perspective.

The socio-economic view makes it clear that people have always grouped themselves around special benefits. It follows that "green offers"—if they want to reach as many prospective buyers as possible—are also subject to defined rules of social community building. The laws of action for the successful implementation of a service in the public sphere are universal: regardless of whether it is a small social institution or a huge amusement park.

Is this another of the numerous brand guidebooks or a new trendy LOHA characterisation (two types of books that are now published on a monthly basis)? No! This is not an *"I'm-an-experienced-consultant-and-this-is-how-one-does-it" work* that destroys a brand's unique identity in favour of supposedly ironclad market and industry rules. On the contrary: You receive a highly individual and directly applicable practical aid for overall strategy and day-to-day business on a sociological basis—with a long-term guarantee: brand sociology borrows its basis from the knowledge of the constant behavioural patterns of individual people, but above all of human interaction. Laws are just as valid in the age of social media and networks as they were hundreds of years ago. This scientific approach deliberately tackles the rampant destruction of values in green companies and aims to dispel the widespread uncertainty there about brand, brand management, and brand leadership. In our experience, successful green companies in particular are often unsettled because, once they have achieved a certain level of success, they are told from the outside that it is now time to do "proper" marketing and "proper" branding. Most of the time, following this advice leads to the opposite.

When we started the "wooden radio" project in 2006 as an "affair of the heart" alongside our main job as brand consultants—as a practical test of our theoretical skills on the concrete object, so to speak—we did not realise that we were becoming part of a development that was intensively picking up speed at the time: Appealing design and green corporate philosophy were suddenly buzzwords that were being reported on in the media: "Ecodesign" was the buzzword under which the developments were subsumed. Product categories, awards, and business models emerged year after year, helping us turn a small wooden radio by Indonesian designer Singgih Kartono into a small but mighty "global icon". We built a brand step by step—implementing our brand sociology consulting practice: sales, brand management, communication. Everything had to be defined from scratch—without venture capital or backers, solely from the proceeds of day-to-day business. Between the years 2008 and 2010, we had waiting lists pages long for the purchase of a hand-built, analogue radio. Journalists not only made their way to us in Hamburg to understand the phenomenon of "wooden radio", but they also travelled to Java with camera teams to get to know and understand Singgih Kartono and its work and product philosophy on site. In the meantime, the waiting lists have been worked off and wooden radio has disappeared from the major magazines, but the brand is alive and well and is considered a blueprint for a functioning green economy.

As brand sociologists, we asked ourselves if we could identify patterns: Who operates successfully as a green brand over the long term and why? From this question, the study of green brands developed far beyond our wooden radio. We found that there were numerous analyses of "LOHA marketing", i.e. the supposed target group, but no well-founded study of the social dynamics of green branding. Thus, this book is now the second step: First, we had to build up and stabilise a "green brand" in terms of brand sociology. Now it is a question of making the insights gained, coupled with our expertise for green companies, generally usable. In order to make this comprehensible, this book contains the following main topics:

- A trenchant analysis of the green market and its players.
- An introduction to brand sociology as a practice-oriented science.
- An exemplary application of the theoretical findings using the example of the brand wooden radio, in order to give recommendations for action for the development and construction of green brands on this basis.
- Six regularities of green brand management condense the results in conclusion.

At the same time, we know that the analysis of green consumer culture made here can only give an abbreviated account of developments and their protagonists: The subject area of "green consumer culture" would require its own well-founded publication, which surprisingly does not exist to date, although the market as a whole is growing. Here, we should refer to the Hamburg-based magazine *enorm*, which comprehensively observes the German-speaking green business scene. In this context, it was important for us to present the origins of green products and their comparatively recent history in order to better understand current successes, resistance, and misunderstandings.

With the explanations of the concrete application, the reader gets an insight into the sociologically based brand analysis, which can be transferred to any company according to its structure. In times when many brands fall victim to the fraying caused by their own management in order to be attractive to every person on the globe and general marketing trends are adopted without checking for individual brand coherence, the "Success Profile of the Brand" offers the definition of a genetic brand code, i.e. an unambiguous system of coordinates. It forms the antithesis to the often shape-destroying 24/7 competitive observation, alien-like benchmarks, and contextless number affiliation. A basic rule of brand sociology is: brands are always destroyed from the inside, never from the outside.

Since we have been working in this field, we have noticed, regardless of the industry, how desperately company and brand managers search for well-founded parameters in order to decide on questions of sales design or even just the design of an advertising poster on the basis of "values" other than the observation that the competition is "already doing this super successfully" (apparently). And in the process, decision-makers are exposed to a Babylonian confusion of offers in the area of brand management: Currently, there are 88 brand evaluation models in the German-speaking world alone. Each of them claims to be the only reasonable one. One thing is certain: In many other areas of science, there is always only one model.

Ergo: 87 existing brand models seem to be wrong; otherwise one would have been sufficient at some point. Brand sociology is not a model, but a strictly scientific analysis of cause and effect.

Last but not least: There are people who have social talent and whose profession enables them to do very concrete good for other people or for nature. In brand sociology, this connection is not automatically given or recognisable, as is the case, for example, with a dedicated teacher, doctor, or social worker. The task of building wooden radio into a brand throughout Europe gave us the unique opportunity to use our profession in a particularly meaningful way: Today, more than 30 young people on Java have a job with a secure future, and some people in Europe know that ecodesign does not necessarily come from Stockholm, New York, or Paris, but also from a small Indonesian village, and can meet the highest international aesthetic standards. As for the sometimes rocky road to the Europe-wide implementation of this idea, which took us almost around the entire globe and let us meet many very special, very committed people, we are grateful and in quiet moments a little proud.

Working on the wooden radio project has given us a deep and extensive insight into the green industry. Fortunately, as a personal "passion project", the small company developed in a commercially positive way, so it was possible to have horizon-expanding conversations with green believers, early activists, and young enthusiasts over many years. All were characterised by a strong personal conviction and history that they associated with their project. Against this background, this book will also be about clarifying the brand strategy of wooden radio and using this example to shed light on "typical" strategy issues in terms of brand sociology. The wooden radio story therefore occupies a special place in the following considerations—as an ideal and professional starting and end point.

Even if brand sociology provides every entrepreneur with structures and dynamics to anchor his performance, the brand origin is always characterised by the fact that people want something at all costs—despite or precisely because everything and everyone speaks against it. The fact that a hand-built radio can develop in a commercially healthy way in times of "galactically" functioning high-end technology, which can often be purchased much more cheaply, is impressive proof of the power of the individual human will to create: Singgih Kartono was determined to place this radio in a world full of radios, and we were allowed to help him with the "birth" of the wooden radio. It remains to add that any good brand management, i.e. one that is strictly oriented towards the long term, makes an important contribution to a healthy economy. Such ventures ensure that people are paid a decent wage for their work so that they can feed their families—all over the world.

Contents

About the Authors

Oliver Errichiello is professor for brand sociology and brand management at the University of Applied Sciences and Arts Mittweida, lecturer for brand management and brand sociology at the University of Applied Sciences Lucerne and the University Hamburg. He is co-founder and managing director of the *Büro für Markenentwicklung* Hamburg. As director, he heads the innovation lab of Deutsche Seereederei, a medium-sized tourism and hospitality company (A-Rosa, aja, and Henri Hotels).

Oliver Errichiello has written numerous specialist books on the subject of brand management and is regarded as an experienced consultant for questions of value-added oriented advertising and as a specialist in questions of "green brand innovation management".

Arnd Zschiesche is a brand sociologist and expert for the strategic management and long-term oriented implementation of brands. He is co-founder and has been managing director of the *Büro für Markenentwicklung Hamburg* for 15 years. Since 2006, 82 brands have been analysed there and operational recommendations have been made for 122 brands. In addition, Arnd Zschiesche has held a lectureship in brand sociology and brand management at the Lucerne School of Business since 2011.

He is the author of 16 non-fiction and specialist books on brand management and is continuously represented in the media as an expert and interview partner (including ARD Markencheck, Plusminus). In his keynotes, he takes a striking stand on everything that goes wrong in brand management.

www.buero-fuer-markenentwicklung.com

Challenges of Green Brand Management

1

Abstract

Green companies have to act successfully in business terms if they want to survive in highly competitive markets in the long term. Against this background, the question arises as to the relationship between economy and ecology in day-to-day business and how companies can "sell" themselves professionally without compromising their green credentials. In addition, there are numerous companies that use "green commitment" superficially as a so-called "hygiene factor", but do not change their actions structurally. This makes it all the more important for green companies to skilfully orchestrate their authentic actions and performance history in order to clearly differentiate themselves in times of unmanageable offers and the eco-social mainstream. Instruments for this form of commitment-based marketing are offered by brand sociology. In a scientific analysis, brands are not freely chargeable products, but cultural bodies that are subject to clear effective social laws of strengthening and weakening. Equipped with this set of instruments, a brand can be controlled "green" according to plan and thus fully develop its value-creating power.

When we were working on and researching the first edition of this book in 2016, the best "green brands" had been selected a few years earlier by a global strategy consultancy. Car brands topped the list of Best Global Green Brands at the time. Now, the reader may think of an innovative company such as Tesla or Deutsche Post's Streetscooter, which was once celebrated in the media (but has now been discontinued), and not so much of the familiar combustion dinosaurs of the industry. However: Ford, Toyota, Honda were the "most environmentally friendly brands in the world" (self-description) in 2014. The winners were actually car manufacturers, companies that mass-produce things that can't avoid—at least until today—consuming precious resources and significantly impacting the environment. After 2014, this award was discontinued—there is no word on the reasons why. One can only guess

© Springer Fachmedien Wiesbaden GmbH, part of Springer Nature 2022
O. Errichiello, A. Zschiesche, *Green Branding*,
https://doi.org/10.1007/978-3-658-36060-3_1

at them. Even then, the question arose: is an exemplary organized waste separation at the company headquarters enough for a green positioning, if gasoline-powered cars are built in the main? What about weapons or fur farms whose production is CO_2-neutral?

In 2019, the US business magazine Forbes announced the most sustainable companies. Result: The Danish company Hansen Holding in first place, followed by Kering SA from France as well as Neste Cooperation from Finland in third place (see Forbes 2019). You don't know all three companies? Probably almost every reader has this experience (Hansen is a biotech company, Kering is the holding company behind such well-known consumer brands as Gucci or Alexander McQueen, and Neste is an oil refiner). The criteria that led to this award are many and varied: they range from a balanced ratio of men and women in management, the purchase of raw materials from responsible sources or a technical transformation away from conventional methods towards resource-saving machines and technical solutions. Here, too, irritation may be in order.

The key question is therefore: How is "green" defined in business? What exactly is a "green" company? It sounds like a simple question, especially in view of the fact that nowadays hardly any company, regardless of its economic importance, can ignore "green values". Meanwhile, the who's who of major national and international environmental awards read like the membership list of relevant brand associations. Are SAP, Vaillant or Otto, Kärcher, Fischer Dübel, Deutsche Telekom, TUI, Tchibo, Procter & Gamble (all winners of the German Sustainability Award) really as "green" as, for example, an Alnatura organic supermarket, GLS Bank or the organic dried fruit supplier Keimling? Why is the internationally respected environmental design prize INDEX, awarded every 2 years by the Danish Crown Prince, primarily given to large multinational companies such as Philips?

Economist and founder of the Alternative Nobel Prize, Jakob von Uexküll, points out that crucial green innovations rarely originate in large companies. Rather:

> Medium-sized companies are generally much more likely to think outside the box and manage with a longer-term perspective. This is also due to the fact that the management of the companies is closer to the people. Both to the reality of their employees and to that of the customer. The pressure to present huge, almost unreal growth rates every quarter and to increase 'shareholder value' is most prevalent in multinationals. Importantly, however, any marketing can only be as green as the product it stands for. (Peymani 2009, p. 22)

In many a company, green corporate activities also have a psychological role for the workforce: "We also do good"—so the classic, less green business can continue undisturbed and with a better conscience. Even small companies that stand as protagonists for species-appropriate animal husbandry and chemical-free agriculture do not have to act completely well per se. For there is a strange contrast in many a business between a high "organic claim" and a ruthless exploitation of committed employees (cf. Bergmann and Lang 2016).

1.1 Green Biodiversity

Under the term "green" seems to exist a variety of different ideas. The color stands diffusely for: good to the environment, to plants and animals. And: concerned to pollute the environment as little as possible. What exactly this implies remains debatable. Certainly, large companies have also pursued "green brand policies" over the past three decades and have contributed significantly to the increased implementation of environmentally and human-friendly technologies and manufacturing methods, and yet the previously undertaken compilation of extremely diverse "green" companies reveals the wide range of sustainable brand policies. The problem is that if so many different things are expressed today by the terms green, ecological or sustainable, then the effect is precisely that there is no clear public image and no unambiguous collective idea of what green is. This is all the more astonishing because green ideas have meanwhile arrived in the much-vaunted "middle of society" and are part of "good manners". Often, in the long term, it remains just "good manners" or, as one managing director put it in a closed meeting: "The thicker the sustainability report, the more dirt behind it . . .". One thing is clear: Sustainability reports are always legitimation documents. The CEO of a billion-dollar company once put it this way: "Environmental protection is a hygiene factor today . . ."—not only with regard to the public, but also as a serious factor for the so-called "war of talents", i.e. the recruitment of employees, since the as it were certified confession of being a sustainable company is more socially desirable and attracts potential (young) employees than companies that have a dubious reputation.

And yet: in 2016, the United Nations General Assembly adopted the 17 Sustainable Development Goals (SDGs), which define the guidelines for politics and business in various areas (peace, food security, climate change and the environment) by 2030—with accompanying funding and economic incentives.

The so-called "green transformation of society" is also being pushed politically at the European level: In December 2019, EU Commission President Ursula von der Leyen announced the "European Green New Deal". The key point: Europe will become a climate-neutral continent by 2050, with renewable energy sources, highly innovative basic research and the protection of regional ecosystems being the guiding principles of business and politics—strongly supported by funding and investment programmes. Even if the effects of the Corona pandemic have weakened these announcements in the immediate aftermath and postponed the timetable, the "deal" as such remains the declared goal.

Exactly the described complexity of ideas about "green" is both a curse and a blessing. On the one hand, the wide range of ideas about a green world means that companies can no longer do whatever they want in this respect. The environmental regulations of the last 30 years nowadays leave hardly any official loopholes for environmentally harmful behaviour, at least in Europe. There has been a noticeable institutionalised cultural change. Environmental impacts are no longer a private or corporate matter, but must now also contend with the sensitively heightened perceptions of customers and the public—sometimes even with unjustified eco-hysteria: Even some of the companies identified as malicious by the media can actually make the observer feel sorry for them in the event of a rampant "wave of indignation". Psychologically, this can only be explained by a collective shift of an individual bad conscience to an external actor.

In addition, the individual range within the ideas makes it clear that almost everyone can currently claim to run a "green company"—perhaps because there are organic vegetables in the company canteen every day. The VW scandal on emissions has revealed how much "green thinking" is used to gain market advantages—without actually acting "green" (in the sustainability report published shortly before the scandal was revealed, VW wrote that its goal was to become the most sustainable car manufacturer in the world by 2018). With the consequence of irresponsibly putting at risk the brand trust that has been painstakingly earned over generations. Among Asian suppliers of European companies, it is fashionable to write an "Eco" in front of the name, to dye the logo green or at least to integrate a cute little animal into the advertising design. It is well known: European shoppers like that. What is called "greenwashing" in Europe, resourceful Asian entrepreneurs know very well how to implement in their own sales-promoting way.

In short: Green stands for everything today and is therefore a zero statement. For example, when McDonald's suddenly switches its M logo, which has had a red background since 1968, to green. Or when AIDA Cruises calls itself a "Green Cruising" company, although only one of 13 ships has been converted from heavy oil to (fracking) gas. H&M managers "produce" as a matter of course punch lines like "Sustainability is not a trend, but the essence of H&M" and offer their "Conscious Exclusive Collection", perfectly exploited in terms of PR, in 150 of the 3500 H&M stores . . . a drop of green. One might like to dismiss this form of argumentation as dubious sophistry, but the discussion about genetically modified seeds makes the conflicting goals clear: Is it "green" if genetically modified seeds become more resistant to diseases, which would lead to a reduction in fungicides in agriculture, for example?

1.1.1   Green Wish Concert?

Accordingly, only very little is supposedly clear under the label "green". And that which is apparently clear is subject to an impressive pressure to forget. Sociologist Joachim Radkau draws attention to this: "The history of the eco-era is not only the history of a new enlightenment, not only a history of knowledge, but also a history of forgetting. Many names that once seemed to embody the future are now unknown even within the eco-scene; countless books that moved people for a short time have long since ended up in junk." (Radkau 2011, p. 614).

This vagueness became particularly clear to us when work began on the "Magno wooden radio" project, the radio made extensively by hand: What is a "green" product allowed to do? What does the audience expect? Who determines when it is "right" to act in the interests of people and the environment? Is an "environmental certificate" the silver bullet and does it relieve the conscience in a publicity-effective-way? There are a thousand answers to these questions, but all in all they prove the following: There is no single way to run a green company. True to the saying that "experiences are always mistakes made", it is only possible to develop one's own idea of how a brand can be built in such a way that it places the environment and people in a positive relationship with a product by constantly testing possibilities and options.

1.1.2 "Making Money" as a Green Problem

The social tension seems to have been clarified and is part of every ministerial Sunday speech: economy and ecology must and must not be mutually exclusive in times of noticeable environmental damage. This is actually a matter of course, and yet reservations can still be felt, especially among people with an environmental conscience, if a company is prospering economically while at the same time aggressively communicating green activities to the public. This is also the experience of Stefan Schulze-Hausmann. In an article, the chairman of the German Sustainability Award Foundation explains:

> Anyone who earns money with sustainability is suspect to some representatives of the pure doctrine. Those who earn a lot of money with sustainability are also a thorn in the side of all those who want to do the same, but are not as fast or as good. And companies that do not care about sustainability issues at all or only to a limited extent have no interest in recognizing achievements that make them seem backward themselves. And then there is the resentment of the active small against the active large, which disregards appreciation for their—in relation to size supposedly manageable—commitment. The big ones, in turn, ignore the 'minimal' steps of the small ones. (Schulze-Hausmann 2012, p. 46)

The Managing Director of Wala Heilmittel GmbH, under whose umbrella the Dr. Hauschka cosmetics brand is produced, summarises: "We need profit. An aversion to profit is nonsense." (Muuß 2011, p. 72).

Against this background, the "sufficiency concept", as advocated by the economist Niko Paech, has taken on a significant role in the scientific-economic debate: Sufficiency poses the question of what is the right measure, what is sufficient, to lead a good or successful life. Is it enough to "reposition" the economy by switching to greener production and distribution methods instead of conventional ones? Does it really solve global problems if we now drink the same amount of an ecologic soft-drink instead of Coca-Cola? Is it better to buy an organic apple from New Zealand than a conventional apple from the local market? Will the environment be saved if 7 billion people own a Fairphone? The idea of sufficiency questions the omnipresent dictum of constant economic growth. In this debate, the question of individual self-realization is transferred from material possibilities of development to immaterial levels—and still shakes the basic cultural values of modern society (cf. Paech 2012).

Even today, it seems that many green companies are reluctant to report on what they do. If they finally decide to do so, the unedifying experience is that renowned external marketing professionals are brought in, who bring in their corporate know-how and their international network relationships, but hardly perceive anything of the independent-individual culture of the company entrusted to them, let alone (want to) consider it sensitively in the strategy management. The saying often used among professionals that one works "on" a brand instead of "in" it is not only a competent-sounding saying, but unfortunately can be understood in the same way in terms of content. The essence of a brand is not captured—at best its shell. The result is green companies that present themselves as perfect in terms of communication, but soulless and interchangeable—companies that engage in communication that has nothing to do with the real thing. In short: marketing takes place separately from the value chain. Marketing as an island of communication within the company. Marketing in a vacuum. Brands that lose their decisive value thanks to this approach: their authenticity.

The economic consequences are usually fundamental: The green regular customers no longer recognize their brand because of the carefully professionalized appearance, and the targeted new target group, perfectly analyzed in numerous surveys, does not believe the different appearance because it collides with the existing expectations, with the positive prejudice against the introduced brand. In the end, the brand destroys its own reason for existence: its unique brand image with clear boundaries—because brand is always commitment. Thus, the green brand icon "Weleda", in the course of a reorientation aimed at "younger target groups" (combined with the purchase of experienced managers from the classic consumer goods industry), came to initiate advertising campaigns that were highly professional and modern, but unfortunately no longer had anything to do with the actual genetic code of the brand and thus the expectations of the clientele. With the catchy slogan "Shower with me", the brand was supposed to appear modern, erotic and attractive—just like all other shower gel brands. Customers no longer had a chance to recognize their brand: The brand makes itself unrecognizable to its backers(!). Before "professionalization", many of these ventures intuitively did a lot of things right—often it was only for this reason that the brand reached that critical size in the first place, at which the owners felt compelled to introduce this kind of professionalization from the outside.

1.2   Brand Is Modern Home

Just like the characterization "green", the term "brand" is unfortunately also a mental wishful thinking in many places: For a good 20 years now, the professional management of brands has been en vogue beyond the professional public. Book publications on the subject as well as search queries on Google under the keyword "brand" have been increasing exponentially since the 1990s. Why? Every company would like to be a strong brand. Even associations, political parties and now even churches conduct workshops such as analyses on the topic of "brand strengthening" and wish to be "anchored in people's minds". "People as a brand" is not only the title of numerous seminars, but also the content of job application training. There's no question about it: brand is considered the last bastion of stability in times when family relationships only encompass "life stages", when religion, apart from

Christmas mass, hardly fulfils any identity- or community-forming function. Traditional hierarchies and values are increasingly dissolving. Neither the family nor the continuity of classical marriage endure. The threats have become global, ecological catastrophes such as Chernobyl or Fukushima or pandemics such as Covid-19 have shaken the world as a global community in its belief in technology—at least temporarily.

Brands are precisely for this reason securing orientation buoys in a confusing world—for many people even the only ones, as it appears in some places, e.g. in Kitzbühel when reading the large-scale signage of clothing utensils. Clothing seems to be particularly striking as a brand carrier, but also in the segment of so-called "fast-moving consumer goods" such as beverages it can be observed that the profane consumption of a water or a lemonade is a political statement: Coca-Cola or Fritz Kola? Lemonaid or Sprite? Even the simple consumption of a bottle turns us into perceived world savers (quote from the drugstore Budnikowsky: "Every purchase is a climate decision") and philanthropists ("Drinking against racism"/"With hops, heart and attitude"—slogans of Littfassbrause). In times of acceleration, a good Karma thus costs a little more than a euro.

But it's about more than just demarcation and belonging to a group: the familiar daily newspaper, the jam on the breakfast table—all laid out by us to stay, to create a sense of being at home. Home is where we know the people and the things, where we can let ourselves go without thinking because everything is hopelessly-joyfully familiar: a thanksgiving of boredom.

At the same time, it is repeatedly suggested that modern people consume in new and different ways every day, and in a deeply individual way. The "producing consumer" has long since taken over the economy. Everything is changing, nothing stands still. On closer inspection, this is all just a myth, but one that permanently fuels and thus drives the marketing machinery. In reality, about 80% of the products that are in our shopping cart are the same products that were there a year ago. Out of 500 new products launched each year in the fast moving consumer goods space, 95% don't survive the first year. A look in the wardrobe reveals strange things: we wear only 20% of our clothes 80% of the time. Advertising expert Klaus Brandmeyer noted as early as 1995: "Communication with the target group will always be difficult if marketing and sales managers can't get out of the ivory towers of their corporate headquarters." (Brandmeyer 1995, p. 22). Much of what is casually characterized as a process of social change turns out, on closer inspection, to be the wishful thinking of a hip (marketing) elite and an equally hip upper middle class in London, Berlin, New York, Tokio Zurich and Paris, who sip their green smoothies at bare stainless steel counters, pull cress and chop parsnips.

The willingness to embrace new things is not an anthropological constant, even in the twenty-first century. Instead, the following applies: Choose what you know. Strong brands are memory anchors, identity founders and, in the best case, a tangible home in a time in which the world knowledge of 10 o'clock at 4 o'clock is already outdated, as sociologist Hartmut Rosa writes. He draws attention to a dramatic social development: "The experiences, practices and bodies of knowledge of the parents' generation are becoming increasingly anachronistic and meaningless for the young, even incomprehensible, insofar as knowledge is tied to participatory practice—and vice versa. The world of Gameboys, the Internet, and text messaging is as incomprehensible and alien to many parents, and even more so to many grandparents, as the customs and practices of a geographically distant culture." (Rosa 2005, p. 187). This leads to a change in the understanding of the generations: "The institution of the 'wise old', which is taken for granted in traditional societies and which is accorded a prominent status because they have 'seen and know everything' and can therefore no longer be surprised by any of life's adversities, has practically disappeared in late modern society: The elderly are instead stigmatized by the fact that they no longer know their way around and that they can no longer keep up." (Rosa 2005, p. 188).

Change and restlessness have become imperatives of life's reality since the nineteenth century at the latest. Even our time off—whether it is a weekend or a sabbatical—is not meant to invite us to idleness, but to help us change perspectives, to create space to tackle new projects or to regenerate for upcoming tasks. Philosopher Ralf Konersmann demonstrates that the view of restlessness and activity as socially desirable as opposed to idleness is no more than 200 years old: "On the one hand, restlessness is an evil because it is immoderate and undermines all our efforts to be one with ourselves and to live in peace. It is restlessness that persuades us that stagnation is a setback and that comfort is suspect. On the other hand, restlessness is our opportunity, for after the failure of the supernatural powers, it alone vouches for the promise of new beginnings and completion." (Konersmann 2015, p. 239).

1.2.1 Restless and Homeless Through Life

Critically, our era is characterized by the withering away of the traditional notion of shared experience: the inexorable global rise of branded goods can be explained sociologically, among other things, by the fact that, with the breakdown of traditional cultural systems, the marked product took over their role. As anthropologists Ryan Mathews and Watts Wacker point out, "The collapse of the traditional understanding of community has not diminished our need for social inclusion. Rather, it has opened the door to neotribalist marketing strategists, companies like Harley-Davidson and Starbucks, who have come to understand the importance of building communities." (Mathews and Wacker 2003, p. 255).

The desire for community is transcultural and immanently anchored in the essence of human beings. Psychologically, this is traceable to the intuitive-subconscious knowledge of the individual that he is always separate and alone throughout his life—precisely when we feel most connected to others. Georg Simmel, one of the founding fathers of sociology, summed up the sensation of loneliness in a scientific way (even before the onset of the modern lack of support in a globalized world): "Once in its deepest layer of personality, of which everyone feels, unprovably but irrefutably, that he can share it with no one and communicate it to no one, the qualitative loneliness of personal life, the bridgelessness of which becomes palpable in the degree of self-contemplation" (Simmel 1987, p. 223).

The special feature of late modernity is not only a structural lack of commitment, but at the same time an unmanageable number of (short- or long-term) commitment options: Not so long ago, in Westernized culture, there was one God, one church, one faith. Today, people have the option to become followers of almost any religion. Before, people chose between rolled roast and goose leg; today, teriyaki sauce, chicken masala, and jam roots are included in the decision-making process. All areas of human life are relative and are even equated by law within an ideology of equality, i.e., they are therefore equally orienting and, in sociological terms, therefore disorienting (cf. Errichiello 2019). The result is fatal: the twenty-first century offers no fixed structures and fixations due to the unmanageable amount of offers. As a rule, anything and everything can now be a center. The philosopher Peter Sloterdijk therefore formulates:

> Where everything has become center, there is no longer a valid center; where everything sends, the supposed central sender is lost in the tangle of messages. We see how and why the age of the one, greatest, all-encompassing circle of unity and its bent exegetes has irretrievably expired. The morphological model of the polyspheric world we inhabit is no longer the sphere, but the foam. The current earth-spanning networking—with all its protrusions into the virtual—therefore means structurally not so much a globalization as a foaming. In foam worlds, the individual bubbles are not, as in metaphysical world thought, included in a single, integrating hyper-sphere, but are drawn together into irregular mountains (Sloterdijk 1998, p. 72).

It is precisely in order to cover up a feeling of the greatest loneliness that we permanently undertake attempts to overcome this state, have children who bring us to the end of our strength, but love us willy-nilly in return—and marry again when one feels lonelier in (one's) relationship at some point than ever before. However, these attempts, which are usually doomed to failure, permanently create new forms of community. Philosopher Alexander Pschera points out an interesting analogy when he writes in relation to the Internet: "We do not become lonely people because we are online too often, but we are permanently online because the loneliness of life plagues us." (Pschera 2011, p. 47).

1.2.2 Green Trust Only Comes About Through Reliability of Commitment

Green" in particular can be home, form the social core of a community and become an individual component of identity. There are many people who proudly and visibly wear their Alnatura jute bags and drape their Voelkel juice on the table during important visits. Social exclusion is inherent in every confession: "I am like this—recognise it in my products". The daily visit to a supermarket is—from a sociological point of view—only superficially attributable to a food supply, because it is also a collectively anchored self-assurance. If you like me, you like me . . . On some dating sites on the Internet, you can "match" with the opposite sex via your favorite brands. Everything has a statement: not only the choice of a Rolls-Royce, but also the choice of a particularly inexpensive Dacia brand car is a social statement. Customers also always take ownership of their brands and then refer to the supermarket as "their supermarket", the restaurant as "their restaurant" or the juice as "their juice". In doing so, they are also always talking about themselves: By singling out the chosen, the discoverer also becomes relevant and special. This is precisely why customers are still the most efficient advertising medium (see also Sect. 4.2.2).

And yet: Even if the ecological-social orientation is becoming increasingly important for branded goods, "green" is not sufficient as a sole performance. An ecologically correct orange juice that does not taste good cannot survive in the long run. And no company can live on commitment to a good cause alone. At the end of the day, even the most ecologically or socially committed global project simply has to perform according to the demands and preferences of the time. Even for green brands it is true that involvement per se is not a serious basis for business: about 80% of all business ideas fail. Only if the performance is ensured, the argument of a green company policy is additionally (but then even more) effective—never vice versa.

A scientifically founded engagement with the topic of "green brand management" faces the challenge of working out the actual social contexts that turn a good or a service not only into a brand, but in this particular case into a green brand. Green brands are not the result of a specific graphic appearance, a CI (corporate identity) or advertising (only advertisers are interested in advertising), a carefully formulated and democratically developed corporate philosophy or a well thought-out communication strategy. They are the result of a social process which in the end ensures that people develop collective trust in a particular name. To this end, it must be made clear what motivates people to place their trust in an offer on a long-term basis or even "blindly". In all clarity: Trust does not develop in commodity markets "somehow" and not via the clarification of "trust" in the sense of nice pictures. Trust is a normative commitment context—a social process: it only arises when a company acts reliably and consistently delivers on its predicted performance. So simple, so difficult.

▶   **Ergo**
   The social dynamics of trust building are at the heart of any well-founded i.e. long-term brand development. Such an approach starts at the causes of green branding and does not try to follow fashions or trends. Brand management based on brand sociology is timeless because the underlying complex social dynamics are cultural laws.

1.2.3   Long-Term Oriented Brands Do Not Tell (Advertising) Lies: Green- and Bluewashing

The repeatedly and justifiably criticized approach of companies to present themselves as "green", while continuing to work exclusively according to classic economic indicators, cannot be explained by malice alone. "Greenwashing" is the term used to describe a form of product and advertising communication that overemphasizes a commitment to the environment, conceals negative effects of the core business, or claims social activities—without factual redemption. In other words: The term "greenwashing" defines activities by companies to create an ecological image through marketing or public relations tools without actually committing to environmental protection. It is therefore opportunistic deceptive behaviour that exploits the public's lack of information (examples are regularly published by the association "Lobby Control"). I n addition, the term "bluewashing" is also used. This is about whitewashing social conditions. Bluewashing refers to the blue colour of the UN, which is used to describe moral diversionary manoeuvres with regard to social engagement. Voluntary initiatives (e.g. the UN's Global Impact Initiative) do promote a commitment to social and legal compliance by companies. As a rule, however, compliance is not monitored and does not entail any legal obligations, but is used offensively by companies for advertising purposes.

When Lidl claimed a few years ago that it was committed to "fair working conditions worldwide", the German consumer protection agency immediately proved to the company that Lidl's working conditions were catastrophic in reality. Lidl then signed a cease-and-desist declaration. The "greenwashing" is an expression of a marketing attitude that believes brands are freely rechargeable social surfaces that could stand for lifestyle today and ecology tomorrow. It's all a question of communication strategy. The carefully cultivated delusion of the miraculous conversion of companies to green pioneers is an overarching phenomenon, if one considers, for example, the ever new attempts by companies to suddenly reach a new target group with communicative crowbars: C&A is suddenly selling Lagerfeld and Lidl is posing as a mega-hip fashion and delicatessen temple. Explicitly related to the area of sustainability, C&A sets an inglorious example: although the company sees itself as the largest supplier of organic cotton, this does not mean that the entire product range is made from organic cotton. Currently, only underwear, basic goods as well as baby clothes are made from organic cotton, using the term "sustainable cotton". However, this does not include the premium organic standard, but a less stringent license under the title "Better Cotton". In doing so, the rubric heading "Organic Cotton" is communicated, approvingly accepting that consumers equate the term "sustainable cotton" with "organic cotton". All this has actually happened, elaborately developed by specialists and plausibly deduced by market researchers. Suddenly a brand—at least according to this management thinking—is cool, young or even green at the push of a PR button, it just depends on the necessary advertising pressure behind it.

Good brand management always has to do with decency and honesty (not only in the green sector): Even an organic seal does not make a "green" brand unless the entire corporate value chain is subject to a comprehensive green performance catalogue. While this belief is widespread in the marketing floors of the world (and feeds this industry), it is wrong in terms of brand sociology. Because the actual brand power is never in the hands of the legal brand owners, but rather in the minds of the people, who in the optimal case, as it were automatically, have positive associations in the same direction when a name is mentioned. The fact that this is the case usually has least to do with advertising: Most brands are not strong because of their advertising, but in spite of it.

▶ **It Applies**
Advertising is one of many different components of brand work—in most cases it is even the least important. No company changes its image (brand sociology: positive prejudice) solely through advertising or a carefully formulated corporate philosophy.

Brand work primarily means dealing with and analyzing the performance level, in all facets that can be directly and indirectly experienced by the customer. It is important to know this performance level *in detail* in order to be able to evaluate whether the potential for a "green brand" exists. Sometimes these prerequisites do not exist—then a company must either decide to continue to focus on other real or currently relevant performance characteristics or to initiate a structured process that creeps in green performance characteristics in a controlled manner and thus anchors this aspect in the long term.

Equipped with a fundamental understanding of collective persuasion strategies and a concrete set of application tools, a brand can be managed "green", free of nebulous declarations of intent, which usually have the character of corporate wish concerts and at best provide short-term employee motivation internally, but do not "green" the company. Green corporate philosophies or *codes of conduct* drawn up in ambitious workshops are laudable, but often only operate on the surface. Most of the time, they are harmless philosophies that are interchangeable and can apply, for example, to a tractor factory just as much as to an eco-shoeshine product.

1.2.4 Purpose Concepts as Added Value

In classical marketing, the view is that products and services would hardly be distinguishable in terms of performance. The special value of a brand would no longer lie in its performance, but above all in perceived values and attributions— image and destination made brands in the modern world. This attribution, also referred to as "added value", means that the focus of communication work is no longer on actual performance, but on "feel-good values" or "emotions" that should create an image. Emotions, however, are highly universal and abstract (which is why we understand them)—brand, on the other hand, is specific. At its core, we trust brands because they are able to solve a problem or task in a characteristic way. No one would think to justify choosing a product on the basis that it would make them "feel good". The dwindling brand relevance is caused, among other things, by an understanding that seeks the persuasive power of a brand outside its task territory. If brands no longer report on their capabilities, why should customers talk about them?

A further reinforcement of this "added value" concept has been the view for some years now that brands could only prevail if they made a contribution to improving the world. Under the concept of "purpose", companies should primarily contribute to solving the great challenges of the time (environmental protection, racism, gender justice). Pepsi does peace campaigns (failed before broadcast), Gillette the new man (failed after broadcast), Dove the natural appearance of women (massive drop in sales), Coca-Cola sponsors Christopher Street Days ("Hate can't celebrate."), to list just a few big players.

This is not new: In the 1980s, the credo of the Italian advertiser Oliviero Toscani (he published a book with the meaningful title "Advertising is a smiling carrion", Toscani 1997), presented with a serious face, provided the first purpose: In his Benetton campaign, Toscani addressed child labor, environmental pollution or AIDS as advertising motifs for sweaters. This was so honourable that the brand was doomed, and it still suffers from the consequences today.

▶ **Let's Hold**

One thing companies are no longer allowed to do on a communicative level: simply fulfill their purpose and earn serious money with it: Profit-shaming.

The position of brand sociology with regard to the en vogue "brand purpose", which asks whether and how sociality becomes a "better place" through the brand (cf. de Chernatony 2001, p. 35), is critical. The communication scientist Julia Frohne distinguishes the two terms "Purpose" and "Brand Purpose" with regard to the groups involved: "A starting point for the distinction between the two terms is offered by a differentiation of stakeholder orientation. While Purpose as a comprehensive term encompasses all stakeholders of the company, i.e. customers, employees, suppliers, local communities and shareholders, Brand Purpose focuses on the shaping of the customer relationship between brand and consumer" (Frohne 2020, p. 29). Frohne concretizes and defines Brand Purpose

[...] as the meaningful raison d'être of a brand, reflected in the inner attitude with which the brand responds to the environment. It encompasses the fundamental values and ethical beliefs of how the brand should be produced, distributed and consumed. The brand lives its attitude by actively working to improve or change social, economic or political conditions and invites its customers to participate in this engagement (Frohne 2020, p. 29).

It is evident that after a phase of "emotionalization" of the brand or image orientation (cf. Burmann et al. 2018, p. 10), the appeal of a brand is now assumed to lie primarily in its "symbolic function" (cf. Kilian and Miklis 2019, pp. 58–65). It is true that in research on the sociology of brands, the brand also assumes the role of an individual identity donor beyond its performance function, but only if the contents have been reproduced in a self-similar and original way over a long period of time and have led to the constitution of a Positive Prejudice (cf. Errichiello 2019). A generalizing "principle of meaning" against the background of socially desirable attitudes, positions and movements (e.g. environmental protection, minority rights) is not suitable for setting distinctive Positive Prejudices and thus resonance perspectives in an unmanageable tangle of segmented communication channels.

In this context, the performance-specific and not image-oriented brand benefits from the social structural change with regard to the intrinsic value of products and services. In his reflections on late modernity, the sociologist Andreas Reckwitz diagnoses that a structural change is taking place that is replacing standardisation with the "logic of the special" in all areas of life (cf. Reckwitz 2018, p. 11). This specialness encompasses the search for the unique, the authentic and the extraordinary. Reckwitz calls this "singularization". Since the 1970s and 1980s, a dynamic has been developing that involves the realization of this claim at all levels of the social: "Singularized are certainly also, but by no means only human subjects, which is why the classical concept of individuality reserved for humans no longer fits. Singularization also encompasses, and to a very special degree, the fabrication and appropriation of things and objects. It affects the design and perception of spaces as well as temporalities and, not least, collectives" (Reckwitz 2018, p. 12).

The collective human being has not changed, but at best the characteristics and personalizations have become finer and more detailed. Things can also be home—especially in times when learned and traditional homes (family, geographical location) are becoming increasingly fragile. Prerequisite: their message character must be uniform and shared so that a collective orientation function can be fulfilled (cf. Errichiello 2019).

1.2.5 Brand Work Is Always Cause Work

Brand work begins where the concrete causes of a group's collective prejudices have their real origins. That is work, not philosophy. Basically, the following applies: Even the myth of an emission-free Tesla electric sports car is still created in a Gigafactory in Palo Alto or near Berlin (cf. Fig. 2.1). And organic goat cheese tastes special because certain goats stand on a certain pasture, eat certain grass and are treated well. This means that brand management as a core area of overall corporate management always starts at the cause level. This requires a determined preoccupation with all performance levels and the unconditional will to immediately eliminate any deviations from the brand promise. In this way, dealing with "soft facts", which is often associated with the topic of brands, becomes hard work with "hard facts" (Fig. 1.1).

This is extremely important, because the trendy topic "green" brings numerous supposed experts on the scene, who all too often promise that one could reposition a brand with a few funny advertisements and a green-colored website (unfortunately not an ironic exaggeration, also applies to the topic brand). In the vast majority of cases this is more than doubtful: How difficult it is to replace a once existing prejudice with a new view has been proven by prejudice research. Brands as extremely stable cultural bodies can hardly be changed, and if so, then only cautiously over long periods of time, but this requires a precise analysis of the brand history from the day of its foundation until today.

Fig. 1.1 Not Palo Alto, but Munich: The electric car BMW 1602. Transport and escort vehicle as well as camera car during the 1972 Olympic Games. Photo: Gudrun Muschalla. (Courtesy of © BMW 2020. All Rights Reserved)

▶ **To the Point**

Green brand management means cause management instead of surface maintenance. This book accompanies you on the way there.

References

Bergmann L, Lang AS (2016) Glückliche Kühe, traurige Menschen. Die Zeit vom 17. März 201613/2016. https://www.zeit.de/2016/13/landwirtschaft-oekobauer-mitarbeiter-ausbeute. Accessed 4 Nov 2020

Brandmeyer K (1995) Schweinebraten ist der Deutschen Lieblingsspeise. Frankfurter Allgemeine Sonntagszeitung 15(10):1995

Burmann C et al (2018) Identitätsgeleitete Markenführung. Springer Gabler, Wiesbaden

De Chernatony L (2001) A model for strategically building brands. J Brand Manag 9(1):2001

Errichiello O (2019) Einsamkeit und die Kraft der Marke. Springer Nature, Wiesbaden

Frohne J (2020) Brand Purpose in aller Munde. Was gilt es in der werthaltigen Kommunikation von Marken zu beachten? Transfer 66, 06. New Business Verlag, Hamburg

Kilian K, Miklis MA (2019) Die Evolution des Purpose. In: Transfer 04/2019

Konersmann R (2015) Die Unruhe der Welt. S. Fischer, Frankfurt

Mathews R, Wacker W (2003) Bunte Hunde. Mit abseitigen Ideen zum Erfolg. Europa Verlag, Hamburg

Muuß CS (2011) Garten Eden in Bad Boll. enorm: 2. Enorm Verlag, Hamburg

Paech N (2012) Befreiung vom Überfluss. Auf dem Weg in die Postwachstumsökonomie, Oekom, München

Peymani B (2009) Vieles ist heiße Luft. Interview mit Jakob von Uexküll. Acquisa 07, Gräfelfing

Pschera A (2011) 800 Millionen. Apologie der sozialen Medien. Matthes & Seitz, Berlin

Radkau J (2011) Die Ära der Ökologie. Eine Weltgeschichte. C.H. Beck, München

Reckwitz A (2018) Die Gesellschaft der Singularitäten. Suhrkamp, Berlin

Rosa H (2005) Beschleunigung. Die Veränderung der Zeitstrukturen in der Moderne. Suhrkamp, Frankfurt/Main

Schulze-Hausmann S (2012/13) Wertschätzung ist Wertschöpfung. enorm 6, Hamburg

Simmel G (1987) Das individuelle Gesetz. In: Das individuelle Gesetz. Philosophische Exkurse. Suhrkamp, Frankfurt/Main

Sloterdijk P (1998) Blasen. Suhrkamp, Frankfurt/Main

Strauss K (2019) The most sustainable companies in 2019. In: Forbes 22. January 2019. https://www.forbes.com/sites/karstenstrauss/2019/01/22/the-most-sustainable-companies-in-2019. Accessed 25 Aug 2020

Toscani O (1997) Die Werbung ist ein lächelndes Aas. Fischer Taschenbuch-Verlag, Frankfurt

Green Consumption

2

Abstract

This chapter describes the hardly manageable multitude of key terms and definitions in the segment of ecologically and socially fair products and services. Against this background, the general characteristics of green brands across different segments are documented and the concept of "green branding" is explained. The overall societal change movements from mass production and acceleration of consumption, via product individualisation and Lohas of the last decades towards a "sustainable economy" are traced and scientifically examined with regard to their economic relevance. Many concrete case studies are used to illustrate how the first green companies pioneered the creation of ecofair goods markets and developed their market positioning or adapted their strategies and offers to a sensitized population in the areas of food, clothing and services specifically in Germany, Austria and Switzerland.

2.1 Clarification of Terms: What Does "Green" Mean?

In the field of green brand management, a multitude of terms are used. All terms are (even today) ambiguous even for experts and unclear or unknown for broad sections of the population. Especially in order not to overestimate one's own actions or one's own level of knowledge and to draw false conclusions, it should be clear that green terms are used inflationary, but have a diffuse meaning for many people or a broader public. In the Allenbach Market and Advertising Media Analysis for Germany of 2020, it became clear that the proportion of people who are prepared to pay more for "environmentally friendly products" is around 25.5 million people (basic population of the German population aged 14 and over)—this is not even half of all potential buyers (cf. Institut für Demoskopie Allensbach 2020).

If one analyses the topic in an academic context, a first, rather inconspicuous publication from 1992 catches the eye. The Briton Ken Peattie from the University

© Springer Fachmedien Wiesbaden GmbH, part of Springer Nature 2022
O. Errichiello, A. Zschiesche, *Green Branding*,
https://doi.org/10.1007/978-3-658-36060-3_2

of Wales published a first textbook for student use under the title "Green Marketing". He points out that the term "green marketing" had already become a "buzz word" by the end of the 1980s, without a well-founded scientific definition. In his publication he closes this gap with the following approach to the object of study. Green Marketing is "The management process responsible for identifying, anticipating and satisfying the requirements of customers and society, in a profitable way." (Peattie 1992, p. VI). The following terms seem essential for activities in the green field: sustainability, corporate social responsibility, organic, fair trade.

2.1.1 Sustainability

The most comprehensive term within the green sector comes up with over 127 million results in a Google search query alone (as of 2020). Influenced by the 1972 Club of Rome report "The Limits to Growth" (Meadows et al. 1972) and the so-called "Brundtland Report" of 1987, sustainability defines the following content: "Sustainable development meets the needs of the present and the necessities of future generations" (Hauff 1987). Joachim Zentes from the University of Saarland (Germany) states that this conception covers three sustainability dimensions: Economic, Ecological and Social (Zentes 2014). All three aspects must be thought of in a balanced relationship to each other and implemented in the corporate strategy in order to realize sustainability in the corporate environment:

- Economic sustainability is when companies do not seek short-term profit at the expense of the environment and people, but act on the basis of long-term corporate goals.
- The ecological component requires the sensible and economical use of accessible resources in order to have workable material in stock in the future. The burdens of production and consumption are to be reduced and a regenerative capacity should be made possible.
- Acting in a socially sustainable manner means taking appropriate account of all the players involved in production.

The above-mentioned model was shaped in a special way by the Enquete Commission "Protection of Man and the Environment" of the German Bundestag in 1998. The three dimensions of ecology, economy and social affairs are considered on an equal footing and treated integratively against the background of the complex interactions between them. The three-pillar model of sustainability is considered to be the most widely used instrument in politics and business. In addition, there are further developments of this model in the form of the so-called "intersection model of sustainability" and the "sustainability triangle" (cf. Pufé 2017).

2.1.2   Corporate Social Responsibility

Another core term in green corporate management is corporate social responsibility, or CSR for short. The first scientists to address the social responsibility of management (and to use the key term sustainabilty) were the US Americans E. Merrick Dodd (1932) and Chester Barnard (1938). Developed further after the Second World War by the US scientist Howard Bowen (1953), the term "CSR" was used for the first time. The core idea is that managers, not organisations, should be responsible. This is because a sense of responsibility is above all a personal inclination and activity. The compatibility of corporate action and a sense of responsibility are central to Bowen. Corporations should be more responsible with their profits than simply providing jobs. More than 20 years later, Archie B. Carroll took this basic idea further and formulated: "The social responsability of business encompasses the economic, legal, ethnic, and discretionary expectations that society has of organizations at a given point in time" (Carroll 1979, p. 500). On this basis, the three-dimensional corporate social performance model (CSP model) emerges. The emergence of the CSR concept in the USA can be traced back above all to the weakly developed welfare state regulatory systems, which presupposed independent entrepreneurial commitment.

CSR today refers to a corporate responsibility and strategy in which ecological and social aspects are incorporated into economic concerns and decisions from the outset. In the diversity of contemporary approaches and definitions, CSR today encompasses the dimensions of economy, ecology, social, voluntary and stakeholder. The European Commission's Green Paper defined:

> CSR is a concept that serves as a basis for companies to integrate, on a voluntary basis, social concerns and environmental issues into their business activities and interactions with stakeholders. (Commission of the European Communities 2001, p. 5):

Today, the term always triggers difficulties of understanding. For "social" can be translated as "social" or "societal". While the first understanding primarily means the isolated responsibility of a company, "social" responsibility implies ecological and economic levels. Against this background, some companies have started to work with the term "corporate responsibility" (CR).

2.1.3   Organic and Biological

Organic farming means "doing business in harmony with nature" (German Federal Ministry of Food and Agriculture 2020). A distinction is made between organic-biological, biodynamic and natural farming. The aims of all three forms of agriculture are to maintain soil fertility, animal welfare and to create the smallest possible nutrient cycle. In order to achieve these main goals, chemical-synthetic pesticides are not used.

The terms "ecological" and "organic" have gone beyond the specialist public and into the general understanding of language and communication. They seem to be the most popular and are identified as follows:

- Organic is mainly used as a term for food from organic farming.
- The term "organic" is a term protected by EU law throughout Europe. The same applies to the terms "from controlled organic cultivation" and "organic".
- Products that are described as "organic" must meet the criteria of the organic seal, but do not necessarily bear the seal logo itself.
- Chemical-synthetic pesticides, mineral fertilizers and genetic engineering are not used.
- The livestock is kept in a species-appropriate manner, no preventive medicines are used—animal meal is also dispensed with.
- Mostly organic farms are controlled: Bioland, Demeter, Naturland, Biokreis are the most important control bodies.

2.1.4 Fair Trade

"Fair trade" refers to a commodity management initiative that promotes greater justice. The idea of fair trade developed at the beginning of the 1970s. The first "Third World shops" were established in Germany at this time. In 1975, GEPA, still the best-known import organisation for fair products, began its work. Fair prices for producers should ensure that people can live in dignity from their work. Exploitative employment conditions—sometimes with the acceptance of child labour—especially in the textile industry cause poverty, because about 90% of all textiles are produced in so-called low-wage countries. The United Nations refers to these people as the "working poor". Fair trade points out these grievances and campaigns for justice and sustainable development opportunities. Through the development of better trading conditions and the implementation of minimum social standards, economic relations are to be made sustainably fairer. Fair trade products are now sold in Germany in 42,000 supermarkets, discounters, organic food shops, bakeries and petrol stations, as well as in 800 world shops, and achieved total sales of €1.6 billion in 2018 (Fairtrade Germany 2019).

It becomes clear that sustainable companies operate on the basis of a large number of different definitions. In addition, gradations and individual definitions apply within these categories. For example, the question of when a food product is actually organic or an item of clothing is fair can be answered differently from one certification seal to the next. Each certificate comprises different criteria and parameters, which repeatedly leads to discussions as to which certificate is "authentic" as opposed to the exclusively "marketing-relevant firmings". According to estimates by the sustainability platform Utopia, there were already around 800 different eco, organic and sustainability seals in 2018—in Germany alone. According to Utopia, five of these are trustworthy and meet a strict set of criteria. Numerous (large) companies use the trustworthy aura of a seal symbol to develop dubious private seals with equally private ideas about content. The actual task of the seal is torpedoed with such "private company seals", namely to enable an overview through the seal in the confusion of the goods markets and to secure potential customers in their "good", i.e. green decision.

What remains? A brief overview makes the difficulty and the jungle of terms in the green market clear. Everyone and everything wants to be "green" and calls itself accordingly. For the purpose of orientation, many of these self-designations are therefore hardly or not (any longer) usable. However, since a brand means standing up for certain values, the mere use of the terms "organic" or "fair" etc. is becoming less and less attractive—the current triumph of "regional labels" is a result of this development.

Organic Versus Regional

According to a study by development experts Rudolf Buntzel and Francisco Marí, which was sponsored by the organisation "Brot für die Welt" (Bread for the World), labels increasingly lead to the exclusion of local producers: "Most involuntarily", critical consumers become allies of a food industry that "dominates food with standards". And which, in the process, only selectively eliminates poverty, the authors argue. [. . .] But the more global retail chains and supermarket giants with their own production want to secure their raw material bases in developing countries and at the same time distinguish themselves as sustainable, the more market power they exercise there, also with the help of their standards (cf. Grefe 2016, p. 33).

A seal is at best a basic instrument for the quick validation of the "green" claim. Brand power, on the other hand, only emerges when certain ideas are clearly anchored collectively. In the future, it will be all the more important for a company to secure differentiation not through "green categorizations" such as typical key terms or seals, but through concrete and uncopyable proof of performance. Put another way: Companies should simply do good brand work.

Definition of "Green"

Precisely in order to be able to represent the diversity of approaches and criteria in this small but obviously highly fragmented market in a practicable way, the approaches mentioned above are summarised below under the term "green". This is to be understood as a form of entrepreneurial trade and targeted consumption which

1. Resources are consumed in such a way that they can be reproduced in the optimum case or that they can be accessed by subsequent generations,
2. Exposes the environment, animals and humans to little or no pollution,

(continued)

3. Does not regard animals as a means to an economic end, but ensures that they are kept in a manner appropriate to their species,
4. does not dishonestly exploit people and guarantees the people involved a fair wage as well as protection and safety at work and excludes child labour,
5. Pursues long-term economic goals that are not generated at the expense of employees.

Certainly, this definition also contains gaps, however, in this way an overarching framework is to be created in order to be able to evaluate sustainable strategies of companies with regard to brand-sociological dynamics. In this sense, it is not an additional definition within the sustainable sector, but rather a summary of content that ensures a system of coordinates for the evaluation of green activities. The claim resulting from this definition forms the content bracket for the use and structural thrust of the analytical instruments presented.

2.2   Social-Historical Development: From the Anonymous Crowd to the Individual Crowd

Green enterprise policy stands at the end of an approximately 170-year European development in the history of industry, which began in the middle of the nineteenth century. The granting of freedom of trade in Prussia around 1810, the development of efficient machines and fast means of transport led to an expansion of the distribution fields and with them to the possibility of an ever faster production of large quantities, which could be sold quickly in the rapidly growing metropolises and their concentrated demand. Industrialization brought about fundamental changes in living conditions. Within a few decades, people were transformed en masse from agricultural to factory workers. The increase in average purchasing power around 1850 made it possible for entrepreneurs not only to manufacture on demand, but to assume that there would be continuous demand and thus to produce standardized quantities in stock. For ever broader sections of the population, it was no longer just a question of satisfying subsistence needs, but of the first forms of "luxury". The slowly emerging middle class and its consumer behaviour formed the social blueprint for the mass of workers and in this way became an ideal for society as a whole.

In terms of work society, the new era also had drastic effects: Before industrialization, there was hardly any distinction between work and leisure. Leisure as a purpose-free period of time was reserved for the bourgeoisie and the aristocracy. This state of affairs changed in the epoch, affecting production and consumption. The historian Kaspar Maase explains: "Millions left agriculture, the village world, the life order of the guilds or the relative unboundedness of a day labourer's existence. No matter whether they were driven by necessity or curiosity, they now had to come to terms with the strict regulations of industry. No longer the position of the sun and the demands of cattle and field, but factory sirens and clocks henceforth determined their daily rhythms, setting in motion the armies of labor, as they were contemporarily addressed." (Maase 1997, p. 41).

Questions about the type and method of production hardly played a role at the turn of the century. Environmental resources seemed inexhaustible at the beginning of industrialization. Only the so-called *social question* increasingly became the focus of political-social disputes due to the extremely different living conditions between capital owners and the working class. The question of whether it was ethically justifiable to let children work or to set unregulated working hours, which in the end only allowed for the bare necessities of life, was one of the decisive disputes of the time. Precisely because inequality was extremely pronounced, the destitute classes at the turn of the century were primarily concerned with participating in the rising prosperity. This led to an interesting combination of the interests of workers and producers: For for entrepreneurship, expanding potential clientele meant boosting sales at the same time. In other words, the consideration of the social concerns of the mass of the working population and the profit motive of the companies did not structurally contradict each other. On the contrary: in order to increase the profit orientation of the companies, the purchasing power of the population had to be strengthened throughout. The money that was now freely available was to flow into consumption by boosting sales through advertising. This development was only possible after the average weekly working time of 70–100 h (at most skilled male workers usually worked 60 h) evoked serious resistance from the workforce, working hours were shortened and a modest wage—above and beyond the necessities of life—was ensured.

The continuing harsh conditions and obligations of work and a permanent self-alienation could—specifically orchestrated—bring about the search for moments of happiness outside the factory gates: The controlled increase in demand led not only to an increase in production quantities, but also to a supposed individualization of supply. By 1900, a mass market had emerged. Maase has described the development of this new kind of market very vividly:

> A minimum of 'little luxuries' was traditionally part of the lifestyle of the urban and plebeian lower classes. (Chicory) coffee, a piece of confectionery, or a colorful cloth for clothing marked self-assertion in a depressing environment. They anchored the indispensable claim to beauty and pleasure in everyday sensual experience. [. . .] Human beings, it seems, give up their dignity, and with it themselves, if they do not maintain a claim to happiness and the wholly other beyond mere functioning. (Maase 1997, p. 71).

Self-awareness or individualization through consumption seems—from a sociological point of view—a key to understanding the origins of a consumption that has become taken for granted today. Amidst an environment of self-denial, commodities offered the possibility of (supposedly) finding oneself through consumption. Increasingly obligation-free time and a—mostly modest—freely disposable capital allowed for a socialization within which the individual with his or her preferences and desires became recognizable. It was not without reason that the development of the first automatic camera (1888) took place in this period, for suddenly there was a leisure time that was worth capturing. Suddenly something that "I" liked or "I" experienced had meaning.

> The imposition of a capitalist economic system can only be explained against the background of psychological motivations: In an industrial society that sees man only as a means to an end, commodities offer the possibility of becoming aware of one's own desires and preferences, of one's own tastes, and of living independently as an individual on a modest scale.

It falls short of understanding brands and brand advertising, as increasingly happened from the 1970s onwards, exclusively from the point of view of capitalist manipulation. Rather, they are a component within the framework of an obvious change of mindset. A component that is undoubtedly economic-materialistic in nature. Nevertheless, one must ask oneself what would remain of modern man if there were no "the brand". Brands guarantee continuity and coherence—especially when everything else is dissolving. In times without real ties, brands can—structurally speaking—be a home and at the same time realize the mass desire for individuality in numerous areas. This makes them successful—across all cultural boundaries. Even in the Hindu Kush, poor donkeys have been spotted with a painted Mercedes or BMW cardboard logo affixed to their hairy foreheads by their drivers.

However the subject of the brand is personally judged: It works. The social success concept of the brand continues to lead to ever greater differentiation and expansion of the range of products and services offered by companies. With positive consequences for the providers: The rising social level, the growing consumption possibilities and consumption desires of ever broader sections of the population cause great demand pressure at all levels of the merchandise economy.

In terms of brand sociology, the era from 1900 to the 1950s is characterized by the following aspects:

* Brand building: The first mass brands emerge.
* Intuitive advertising and communication work: it is done without significant market research.
* Manufacturer dominance: The brand is in the foreground and is part of everyday life.
* Regional/national distribution: Brands are mostly regionally or nationally known players.

The following becomes clear: Self-realization by means of consumption and the creation of a worthwhile (illusory) reality outside grey factory gates did not evoke any sensitivity with regard to sustainable corporate management in this period. Initially, it was solely about the need to work on one's own "material happiness". Until the 1950s, there was hardly any evidence of "green ideologies" on the part of entrepreneurs or consumers. This was certainly also a result of the fact that resource consumption was still in its infancy and the associated effects, although perceptible, did not seem threatening enough. This observation is quite consistent with psychological analyses of the classical hierarchy of needs, according to which physiological-material desires want to be fulfilled first, before people focus on questions of realization that are superior to them. With the concept of post-materialism, the social scientist Ronald Inglehart developed a structural analysis that can be applied almost ideally to the formation of a modern consumer culture. According to Inglehart, psychological and physical securities form the basis for developmental stages towards an increasingly materialistic society that ultimately strives for individual forms of self-realization. Inglehart (1998) defines the stages as follows:

- Pre-modern societies: The focus is on securing one's own survival.
- Modernity and industrial society: striving for individual prosperity and security.
- Postmodern society: high standard of living across the population; consumer and service society; individual self-realization.

2.2.1 The Green Me

A historical analysis of the green sector reveals a direct link to civil society developments: Around 1961, for the first time, a political party had drawn attention to the issue of environmental protection. The German Social Democratic Party (SPD) under Chancellor Willy Brandt addressed ecological issues under the slogan "The sky over the Ruhr-region must become blue again"—the rapid economic upswing of the post-war years allowed criticism of technology to wither away. However, as early as 1953 philosopher Friedrich Georg Jünger had formulated a radical, fundamental and uncompromising critique of technology in his essay "Perfection of Technology". He wrote—almost visionarily: "Technology does not produce riches; through its mediation, however, riches are brought to us, processed and made accessible for use. It is a constant, ever-growing, ever-more-vast consumption that takes place here. It is an overexploitation such as the earth has not yet seen . . . All theories that disregard this fact have something askew about them, for they undercut the condition under which working and economic activity now take place." (Jünger 2010, p. 28). And, "What is called production here is in reality consumption" (Jünger 2010, p. 29), "a consumption which, if we estimate the whole earth for it, drives overexploitation to the extreme (Jünger 2010, p. 88)." His thoughts go largely unheeded.

More than 10 years later, environmental protection is also taken up politically. A publication by the Federal Environment Agency brashly states that the "Willy Brandt Campaign" marks the beginning of environmental political thinking in Germany. A year later, the first edition of "Silent Spring" is published in the USA. The author, Rachel Carson, warns against the contamination of the environment, animals and humans with pesticides, especially the insecticide DDT (Carson 1987). Carson's bestseller succeeded in making a larger public aware of environmental issues.

The term "environmental protection" appears in Germany for the first time in 1969 in a document from the Ministry of the Interior. In 1971, "Test" magazine reports on "organic" for the first time (Faller 2013, p. 47). It becomes clear that the political debate on "green" does even cover 50 years. In his book "Die Ära der Ökologie" (The Era of Ecology), the social scientist Joachim Radkau states after an analysis: "Most of the individual elements of what today goes under 'environmental protection' already have a long, in some cases very long history under a different name—the more the historian investigates, the longer it becomes. One thing, however, can be stated in advance: More or less new from 1970 onwards were the networking, the broad impact, the global horizon." (Radkau 2011, p. 28). The Club of Rome report "Limits to Growth" (Meadows et al. 1972), which is still widely cited today, and the high-profile publication "To Have or To Be" by Erich Fromm (1976) reached millions of copies and succeeded in sensitizing broad sections of the population to green consumption. Environmental catastrophes such as the "dying of the forests" (1982), the chemical catastrophe in Bhopal (1984), the reactor catastrophe in Chernobyl (1986), the observation of a dwindling ozone layer (in 1988 a scientific report had a broad impact) and the tanker accident of the Exxon-Valdez (1989) off Alaska made the limits of economic growth clear world-wide. A process of rethinking began, which eventually led to political movements of their own; in Germany, for example, the "Greens" entered the Bundestag for the first time in 1983. (The first Green Party "Values Party" was founded in New Zealand in May 1972. In the 1975 national election, it received 5.3% of the votes cast). By the end of the 1980s, environmental issues are of global media interest, dominating collective emotional states and thus promoting their political relevance. The climate summit in Rio de Janeiro (1992) dominates the global ecological discussion into the second decade of the twenty-first century, the "climate summit" in Paris (2015) leads, after numerous failed attempts, to globally accepted framework agreements on climate protection or formulates the declared will to limit global warming. If one critically compares the media impact of the first climate summit in Rio with that of Paris, however, it is equally clear that the broad impact of the topic has a wave characteristic. Thus, the coverage of the Paris results took a few days and only the Fridays for Future movement was able to set the socio-political agenda again around 2019/2020—until the outbreak of the Corona pandemic.

The turn to green consumption strategies is not a trend that flares up for a short time, inspires people and finally fades away, but in its fundamental (over-)necessity for life a constantly topical issue. This is also made clear by the natural scientist and co-author of the latest report of the Club of Rome, Jorgen Randers, entitled "2052". Randers (2016) gives humanity only a choice between managed decline or collapse. Green economic strategies have therefore long since ceased to be a "nice-to-have", but rather, in the best sense of the word, future-proofing for the environment, people and animals, and not least for companies. While profiteers can still be found unscrupulously exploiting the earth's resources (and realizing their practices beyond the sight and reach of well-resourced Western NGOs), in the long run environmental catastrophes and dwindling access to raw materials will necessitate change. No company will be able to refuse "green strategies" ethically, but also economically—at some point it will simply become too expensive.

2.2.2   Start of the Green Idea

In the ecologically oriented public, the emergence of a perceptible green consumer culture is readily located well before the 1950s, but this is primarily an intellectual debate that can hardly be traced in terms of industrial history. For what remains decisive for a general consideration of "green branding" is its real implementation in mass consumption and its fundamental effects on the reality of life of an expanded public. Radkau is even more explicit in his book on the history of ecology: "Already about where the historical beginning of the environmental movement and environmental protection lie, the ideas in the literature diverge widely and range between 1770 and 1970; and even more so the end is completely open." (Radkau 2011, p. 32).

Nevertheless, the first avant-garde thought experiments and individual ecological experiments in agriculture form the basis for an economy that perceives the environment as a subject. The first traces can be found at the beginning of the eighteenth century. Hans Carl von Carlowitz is regarded as the intellectual founding father of the green movement. As chief miner in the Ore Mountains, he was responsible for supervising mining operations, smelters and the working conditions of miners. His later fame since the 80s of the last century in the German-speaking world is connected with his thoughts and the creation of the word for the principle of *sustainability*. Von Carlowitz's professional work coincided with a time of energy shortage, because the consumption of wood by the huts led to a widespread shortage of wood. In view of his experience, the goal in the future should be to manage the forests in such a way that tree consumption and tree cultivation were in balance with each other.

Carlowitz's thoughts stand out from the realities of his time, since at that time the focus was on daily survival and living in the here-and-now. The thought of "tomorrow" was not only strange, but absurd—especially since the large part of the population did not possess anything that they could have passed on to their descendants. The social disposition was also differently poled: earthly life was only an intermediate stage on the way to the eternal kingdom of heaven. Only one group of the population seemed to be in a position to plan the future: the nobility. Carlowitz suggested the principle of "sustainability" to them for economic reasons (securing wealth for the clan), thus initiating an understanding of resources that was oriented towards regeneration and the future. Specifically, Germany became a pioneer of forest reforestation and at the same time (as a by-product) a place of forest romanticism (cf. Radkau 2011, p. 48). Interestingly, the social anchoring of green philosophies of life has hardly changed: Even today, customers of "green" products and services are mostly educated above average and have more financial means than the majority of the population.

When dealing with the topic of "green", agriculture is considered the place of origin of an ecologically oriented economy. A contaminated soil, a deforested forest and sick animals are quickly recognizable and have existential effects on options for action and livelihoods. On closer examination, it is noticeable that, similar to von Carlowitz, whose ideas were related to intergenerational "resource security", the first organic pioneers initially focused solely on the long-term economisation of their agricultural land, i.e. securing soil yields. Green action was not an end in itself in its beginning. The integration of green intentions is hardly driven by the idea of a "better" world, but above all by the question of how farming can be optimised in the long term, i.e. what steps must be taken to ensure that a (farming) enterprise can operate successfully in the long term.

2.3   History of the Organic Sector

2.3.1   The First Makers

Due to the declining fertility of the soil and reduced biodiversity, as well as dubious food quality, biologists, farmers and veterinarians approached the founder of anthroposophy Rudolf Steiner (1861–1925). This inquiry gave rise to Steiner's "ecological" manifesto: the "Agricultural Course" (Steiner 2011), in which he describes each farm as an individual organism that should be subject to its own rules. Orientation towards anthroposophical laws, the use of biodynamic preparations, the obligatory keeping of ruminants and the observance of "cosmic rules" (Eigendiktion) are intended to bring production and consumption into a healthy relationship for humans, animals and the environment. To this day, a large number of organic farms (including the Demeter farms) follow the classical forms of anthroposophically oriented agriculture. Steiner thus played a prominent role in the first organized implementation of "sustainable" production philosophies and at the same time continues to shape the negative public image of ecologists to this day.

One of the first farms in biodynamic agriculture is the Bauckhof in Northern Germany—in 1935 Eduard Bauck founded the first association for biodynamic agriculture. Subsequently, in the middle of the twentieth century, the Swiss couple Hans and Maria Müller prepared an increasingly public basis for organic farming: together with the German doctor and microbiologist Hans-Peter Rusch, the two agronomists are regarded as pioneers of this development. In order to save small farms in Switzerland from giving up their existence, the focus was on self-sufficient forms of farming: farms should operate as independently as possible from external inputs. The main aim was to preserve soil fertility by optimising the farm's own fertiliser: this was intended to reduce production costs in the long term in order to increase food quality and safeguard soil fertility.

However, those pioneers of organic farming cannot hide the fact that the majority of farming continued to be carried out conventionally, and still is today.

2.3.2 The First Forms of Sale

The creation of an ecologically oriented production formed the basis for an equally ecologically oriented distribution. The so-called health food stores and later natural food stores offered a first range of Demeter dairy products, "unsprayed" fruit and vegetables as well as pulses and cosmetics in the 1960s. The first German organic food store is considered to be the "Peace Food" store in Berlin, founded in 1971 (cf. Fig. 2.1). The shop "Schwarzbrot" (founded in 1972) operates in Hamburg, "Ambrosius" in Osnabrück and "Macrohaus" in Münster. The assortment includes grains, flakes, dried fruits and so-called macrobiotic foods. Also in the early 1970s, the registered association "bio-gemüse" was founded, the forerunner of the widespread "Bioland" growers' association for organic food (founded in 1976). In 1975 a wholesale trade for organic products was established and in 1979 the first organic cooperative. In 1982 the "Naturland" growers' association was added. By the mid-1980s, there were already around 2000 producers of organic food in Germany alone, offering around 1000 different items in their "Naturkostnetz".

The beginning of the 1980s is considered a time of growth in the organic sector. The author Helma Heldberg explains: "Thirty newly founded shops per month were not uncommon, the 150 shops at the end of the seventies quickly became 300, the 300 then 500 and so on. For to the pioneering work of the 'conviction doers' and the needs of the 'nutrition freaks' was now added a growing demand due to other events: reports about the destruction of nature and environmental catastrophes, the discovery of the dark sides of industrial society even in one's own body caused a growing sensitivity in the area of nutrition" (Heldberg 2008, p. 18). This was followed by the

Fig. 2.1 Germany's first organic food store: Peace Food Berlin 1971. (Courtesy of © Landesarchiv Berlin 2020, F Rep. 290 No. 0.159.684/Photographer: Ludwig Ehlers. All Rights reserved)

first organic fair in 1983: 55 exhibitors came together. With the triumphal march of supermarkets around the early 1980s, the first organic supermarket is founded in Germany—after the first "organic products" can be found on the shelves of tegut and dm drugstores: Until then, healthy, organic consumption was synonymous with dreary grain food and shrivelled apples. Visually unattractive packaging, coupled with a high-price policy, were the reasons why organic products did not get beyond a niche existence in the natural food and health food sector. Expensive and ugly were characteristics of the organic industry. You had to believe in it to like it … and preferably shop with your eyes closed. Negative prejudices against organic products that still exist today draw their social energy from such collectively anchored images.

2.3.3 Turn of the Century from the 1980s

The Alnatura brand, initially founded by Götz Rehn in 1984 in the city of Fulda opens Germany's first organic supermarket in Mannheim in 1987. Stylistically, the brand is based on a classic supermarket. In the meantime, around 1000 organically produced products are sold under the Alnatura name. Previously, in 1974, the Upper Franconian company Denree (French: denrée = staple food) began to produce dairy products from biodynamic agriculture and to supply natural food stores. The economic success led to the foundation of an organic market group of independent organic retailers and finally to the opening of an own organic market chain, the "denn's Biomärkten" in 1996 (assortment approx. 15,000 products). In 1997 the organic supermarket "basic" opened. The goal of expanding the customer base was met with irritation in the industry: The attempt at that time to cooperate with the discounter Lidl led to protests in the industry and to delivery boycotts by producers.

Until the mid-1990s, however, the majority of organic products continued to be synonymous with products that were unattractive in terms of taste and design and that appealed to a very specific clientele of "ecologists". For example, the company Ritter Sport had to move the organic seal printed on some varieties or their packaging from the front to the back because people did not consider the term "organic" to mean good taste. However, it subsequently turned out that it was now no longer clear to customers why these bars cost more than the usual range. So the organic seal was again put on the front of the packaging. Today, a chocolatier like the Austrian company Zotter, which converted its production to fairtrade in 2004 and to organic in 2006—is considered a premium supplier. All chocolate ingredients—whether whisky or goji berries—are organic.

An outstanding example of very early developments in green business forms is the Upper Palatinate company Neumarkter Lammsbräu. Under the management of Franz Ehrnsperger, the almost 400-year-old brewery experiences a fundamental change in terms of sustainability. As early as 1976, "environment" is defined as a corporate objective and in 1987 the world's first ecological beers (draught and dark) are offered. In 1996, the entire beer production is converted to organic farming. Well before the triumph of the trendy organic soft drinks in the late 2000s, the brand has been offering organic lemonades under the brand name now since 1998.

In general, the penetration of organic products across broader sections of the population succeeded from the mid-1990s onwards. The reasons for this were the expansion of the distribution network of ecologically oriented distributors, a professionalisation of the public image and an increasingly adapted pricing policy, which made it possible for larger sections of the population to buy organic products. The increasing democratisation, diversification and individualisation of the product range finally led to a broader acceptance of organic products, even into the assortment of classic discounters. Klaus Braun, a specialist in the natural food trade, points out: "The manufacturers who supply the trade now think that they have to broaden their ranges and bring every conceivable product onto the market as an organic version. This leads to organic becoming a marketing issue. So if you position your brands sufficiently well, you have the chance that the customer will associate a higher quality with this positive impression—regardless of the actual quality." (Winkelmann 2014, p. 37).

Summary

Basically, it can be stated:

- "Organic" originated in agriculture (as a profit maximizing principle).
- Organic products in the 1960s to 1980s were sold through the niche market of health food and natural food stores.
- The expansion of the clientele began at the beginning of the 1990s, when organic products had a steadily growing distribution network and approached the style of classic products in their appearance and communication.
- From the mid-1990s, traditional supermarkets and later discounters also successively included (price-competitive) organic products in their assortments.

2.4   The Economic Importance of the Organic Sector Today

The share of organic products in total food sales (as of 2019) was 5.68% in Germany, 9.3% in Austria and 10.3% in Switzerland. The market share has doubled in the last 5 years alone. It is interesting to compare these figures with consumer studies. Because about 50% of all Germans state that they pay attention to an organic label when buying food (Federal Ministry of Food and Agriculture 2020, p. 14). Clearly formulated: Even after more than 25 years of spreading the topic of "organic food", it is still a small share of the total market, even if large parts of the population would like to act and buy green in principle and do so to some extent (in the grocery trade, milk, butter and eggs are bought "organic" disproportionately). The reasons for this are manifold, but the decisive point is the still higher price of organic food compared to conventional products—even if this connection is repeatedly negated by observers of the industry. Instead, the lack of supply and overly cautious communication are preferably held responsible for this dilemma.

If we look at experiences from ranges/product areas that have already been addressing the issue of "sustainability" for 10–20 years (food, mobility), a basic problem can be identified: Although the stated willingness for sustainable behaviour and sustainable consumption is very high, the actual implementation is perceptibly lower. This leads to the effect known in market research as the "silence spiral" (cf. Noelle-Neumann 1989) or the so-called attitude-behaviour gap. This means that there is a discrepancy between (formulated) aspirations and reality, or between the desire to act sustainably and the actual actions of consumers: consumers state that they are interested in sustainable consumption, but do not put this into practice. Meanwhile, the underlying causes have not yet been sufficiently investigated. However, it can be assumed that, on the one hand, people give socially accepted and socially desirable answers in surveys and that their answers are therefore not reflected in actual consumption. On the other hand, the occurrence of the aforementioned gap may be due to the fact that consumers are intrinsically motivated to buy sustainably, but certain barriers prevent them from doing so (such as cost barriers). Thus, consumers' actual behavior often differs from their attitudes and intentions due to the many influences. Many different individual, social and situational factors thus influence the factual decision-making process.

The clearly perceptible uncertainty, enriched also by media reports, which increasingly report that organic products are not automatically "healthier" in times of seamless food controls and specifications of all goods, invalidates the decisive argument for the purchase and seems to catch on in terms of publicity. In other areas, too, green consumption is all too often subject to short, trend-dependent swings. Around 2010, for example, hybrid and electric vehicles were positioned as the cars of the future, and it was prominently posited that it was only a matter of time before all the world's passenger cars would abandon gasoline and diesel. In 2014, at the auto shows in Detroit and Geneva that were decisive for the industry, the young technology played only a subordinate role: Instead, SUVs (sports utility vehicles) that displace inner-city space and have the gasoline consumption of combat lift screws were the focus of public attention and the flash of lightning—simply because these vehicles sold best.

Real Consumer Behaviour Using the Example of SUVs
The number of SUVs in the overall German market rose from 9.8% of the total passenger car market in 2014 to 21.1% in 2019—the figures from Switzerland and Austria are similar (Statista 2020a).

- The cliché that hip consumers drive to the organic market in an SUV with an average consumption of 12 L per 100 km does not lack a certain basis.
- The Car-Sharing services constantly mentioned in the media comprise 27,000 vehicles in Germany. By way of comparison, there will be 47.7 million vehicles on the road in Germany in 2020—more than ever before.

Automotive designer Lutz Fügener explains the underlying logic as follows: "The problem is: In the car industry, young people are not very relevant to the market. The younger ones would be interested in innovations, but they don't have the money. The older people would have the money but have no interest." (Grimm 2014, p. 23, 25). Even this thesis could be questioned, after all, the recent study on "Environmental Awareness in Germany 2014" came to surprising results among the age group of 14 to 25 year olds: "Environment and nature play a less important role in young people's ideas of a good life than in the overall sample. While among all respondents 30% consider an intact environment and the opportunity to enjoy nature to be an important part of a good life, in the age group of 14- to 25-year-olds this figure is only 21%." (Umweltbundesamt 2016, p. 12).

Environmental awareness and environmentally conscious action remain two profoundly different spheres and do not seem to be limited to certain age groups. A striking example: the breach of trust, difficult to surpass in its scope, that the VW brand made towards its own clientele and the general public with the manipulation of exhaust gas values, did not (!) lead to a collapse in sales as a result. In July 2017, the Hamburg weekly magazine Die Zeit reported with surprise: "In the first half of 2017, Europe's largest carmaker handed over just under 5.2 million vehicles to its customers—0.8% more than in the same period last year. In June alone, deliveries increased by 4.2% year-on-year to 920,700 new cars, the manufacturer announced in Wolfsburg on Wednesday." (Die Zeit 2017).

It is undoubted that an expanded public is permanently asking questions about the environmental compatibility and social conditions of production. Due to the continuous presence of this topic and an ethical self-assertion of the media, many companies today give themselves a green veneer or at least separately highlight social and/or green aspects of their actions. It remains the case that the discrepancy between today's definitely existing sensitivity and social relevance of the topic and the actual individual actions is still high. As described above: The topic has arrived, only the implementation is still lacking.

However, it is crucial to note that the market for green products does not appear to have increased significantly in size, but that the depth of supply of these products and services is steadily increasing. Meaning? People who buy organic food anyway should be able to realise their green consumption philosophy in all areas of life according to the situation—just as "normal" supermarket shoppers are being supplied by the industry with more and more options, including more organic products. It is also clear that the food retail sector in particular, which is affected by very small margins, is looking for ways to increase its narrow profits through (more expensive) organic products. Only against this background is the market development described below comprehensible.

2.5   Expansion of the Green Consumption Zone

2.5.1   Green Clothing

"Green fashion" is also referred to as green fashion, eco-fashion or eco-fashion. Green fashion encompasses a range of criteria that include production, human, disposal and use ecology as well as social-ethical aspects. Organic cotton in combination with Fairtrade and social commitment are the central and most widespread practices in this segment. It is clear that a move towards "green products" had its origins in the range of food and care products—everything that goes into or onto our bodies. There was a time lag before other product ranges were "greened". Even more limited in terms of economic significance, a market emerged for clothing from sustainable production, although this term did not play a role in the early years of the market. In the 1970s, the segment of "sustainable fashion" was still considered "eco-slouchy look", but in the following years it became increasingly professionalized and aestheticized. One example: the north German company Himalaya has been selling "natural textiles" since 1977. Company founder Alexander Frieborg brought back clothing from trips to India and Afghanistan in a VW van, which he then sold directly at flea and eco markets. The brand became known for the Himalayan reversible jacket, which is still part of the range today—in a contemporary design. The range has become much more fashionable, but patchwork elements and bright colours carry on elements of the hippie early days.

In the mid-1980s, environmental experts began to address the unrestrained use of chemicals in textile production. The first companies tried to produce jackets and trousers in a more environmentally friendly way and used natural fibres from organic farming from the 1970s onwards. Anthroposophically oriented companies such as Hess Natur (founded in 1976) avoided toxins in clothing (cf. Fig. 2.2), Maas Naturwaren emerged (1985) in response to reports of toxic substances in nappies: The founding Maas family offered cotton eco-diapers by mail order, initially shipping them from the basement of their home. Toxin-free clothing for children soon followed. The company now has—by its own account—a customer base of about 1 million people, of which about 520,000 are active shoppers. A consumer study in June 2019 revealed that Hess Natur is considered the most sustainable fashion brand in Germany—followed by the Swiss brand Freitag (Serviceplan Sustainability Study Fashion 2019).

The first suppliers of purely mass-market oriented eco-fashion—in contrast to the individual commitments of farms—were large companies in Germany: The mail-order company Otto, for example, brought out the first eco-collections under the name "Future Collection" at the beginning of the 1990s: chlorine and optical brighteners were dispensed with. (The Otto Group defined "environmental protection" as a strategic corporate goal as early as 1986). Esprit followed in 1992 with an organic collection, and Britta Steilmann, then chairwoman of the Steilmann Group and a trained fashion designer, developed the first German eco-collection around 1990 and was eventually awarded the Federal Cross of Merit for her commitment.

Already at this time the magazine Der Spiegel reported (Der Spiegel 1994, p. 130): "More and more consumers in the Federal Republic feel the same way as

Fig. 2.2 Hess Natur
catalogue: Eco hippster free—
feel good 1985. (Courtesy of
© hessnatur-Textilien GmbH
2016. All Rights Reserved)

she does. Many of them would like to buy environmentally friendly fashion. But they feel overwhelmed to judge all the test seals and badges." (The first environmental seal in the Federal Republic of Germany was the "Green Angel", which has been in use since 1978). The first seals were created, mainly based on the Austrian model "ÖkoTex-Standard 100". This seal is awarded to companies whose clothing does not contain pesticide residues. And yet: the ambitious projects of the large companies all failed. According to an expert on ecological fashion, the blogger and activist Kirsten Brodde, these companies were ahead of the zeitgeist in the 1990s: there was no market for this form of clothing, and in addition the technical possibilities for producing ecologically correct and aesthetically pleasing fashion were limited (Köhrer 2013, p. 23).

A stronger breakthrough of "sustainable fashion" only occurred in the course of public awareness at the turn of the millennium: From the year 2000 onwards, small fashion labels increasingly set up, endeavouring to ensure sustainable production. Kirsten Brodde remarks: "[The small ones] are pushing the big ones. Because they see that there are customers for this small green range, which is not renewed every week. Customers who would rather spend a few euros more on a garment and buy one less in return." (Köhrer 2013, p. 23).

Due to the creative output and the high standards of the small enterprises, even large textile chains increasingly felt under pressure: environmental and social standards were developed, which the majority of all companies voluntarily agreed to. In 2009, during the Fashion Week in Berlin, a "Green Showroom" was organized for the first time by designers Jana Keller and Magdalena Schaffrin with a total of 16 labels. Shortly thereafter, the "Ethical Fashion Show" followed (since 2010—the Parisian precursor already started in 2004). Today, the Innatex trade fair is considered the leading trade fair and order platform for green fashion in Europe.

At the same time, the era of seals and certifications began, which informed potential buyers at a glance about the "certified green" origin of the goods. There are currently around 120 different labels operating in the green textile market. Many of them have to give up after a few years despite great commitment, so that the supplier market is in constant flux. A positive example is the company Armedangels, founded 13 years ago: sustainable design and fashion orientation led from formerly three to now 70 employees. In 2016, the company generated €24 million in sales—with steady growth of 40% per year.

Founded in 2007, the GOTS certificate (Global Organic Textile Standard) is the most successful seal in the global textile market to date, with several thousand affiliated companies. According to its website, its own claim is: "Our mission is to develop, implement, verify, protect and promote the Global Organic Textile Standard (GOTS). This standard sets the requirements for the entire supply chain for both environmental and working conditions in textile and apparel production that uses organically produced raw materials. Organic production is based on agriculture that maintains and restores soil fertility without the use of toxic, permanent pesticides and fertilizers. In addition, organic production relies on appropriate animal husbandry and excludes genetic modification." (Global Organic Textile Standard website: Our Mission, Our Vision 2020).

Parallel to the green fashion labels, the first shops for a modern form of ecofashion also emerged:

- Hamburg-based Uli and Manfred Ott were among the first sellers of eco-fair fashion for women. Their shop "marlowe natur" came into being in 1992—after selling conventionally produced fashion for many years and no longer wanting to conform to the existing production conditions.
- Another pioneer that offered a full range of eco-clothing: "glore" in Nuremberg. The founder Bernd Claude Hausmann, a former professional football player and social worker, was looking for fair and ecological clothing that was nevertheless fashionable, and did not find it in Germany. This initial situation was the founding idea for glore, a business with further "concept stores" in Germany and Switzerland.
- Another variant in the field of ecofair fashion is offered by the Munich company "deargoods". Under the guiding principle "Animal—Human—Ecofriendly", deargoods is the only provider with a total of seven shops that sells exclusively organic, vegan and fair.

It is difficult to measure the share of "green fashion" in the textile retail trade, as there is still no overarching seal that combines the multitude of different assessment criteria and thus ensures what is really "green". According to a GfK study, the share of certified fashion in the sales of the total textile market was around 3.2% in 2013—more recent figures are not available. For the 2017 financial year, the Fair Trade Forum reported sales of €1.5 billion. Fairly produced textiles took about 10% of the turnover. The interest in sustainable fashion is also shown by the number of visitors to international green fashion fairs. Among the largest events in this respect is the so-called Neonyt with 150 national and international exhibitors. In addition, there is the Innatex trade fair. It is considered the leading trade fair and platform for sustainably produced fashion. The number of visitors is increasing.

However, sustainable fashion only takes up a very small share of the overall textile market, which can be extrapolated when the GOTS standard is taken into account. This label expects at least 70% biologically controlled natural fibres.

The Green Fashion Market in Figures

- GOTS recorded a share of 0.12% in the total textile market in 2015, corresponding to €53 million in sales.
- If one compares this sum with the total turnover of the textile market in Germany in 2016, 65 billion, then sustainable fashion does not even account for 1% of the sales volume. However, observers doubt this share, as all labels and self-certifications are included in the assessment.
- The result of an industry survey among eco-certified companies, which have shown a continuous sales growth of about five percent per year for 10 years, while the market of conventional clothing suppliers has been shrinking for years, is confirmed. In reality, the share is many times smaller.
- A Greenpeace study clarifies the reality of life in 2015: three out of four young people are well aware of the negative consequences of conventional textile production (exploitation, environmental destruction, etc.), but only about ten percent pay attention to eco-labels and country of origin when buying (see enorm 2/2015, p. 12).
- In 2019, a study in Germany, Austria and Switzerland revealed that only 11% of all respondents would "often" consider sustainability when buying clothes—24% "never" and 33% "rarely" (Appinio October 2019).

The triumph of highly price-oriented textile brands such as Primark (Primark peaked in 2019 with sales of €7.79 billion, as did KiK with €2.1 billion). This player indirectly conditions market events via the setting of neuralgic price points—"across the board"—the price structure of the markets up to the subjective price perception of the buyers. Primark permanently criticised for their production and social policies, but also for the lack of environmental compatibility of their clothing. This contradiction makes it clear that "eco-fair fashion" is still in a tough battle with the "bargaininess" of offers—especially among young target groups.

2.5.2 Furniture & Construction

In the furniture industry, mass greening or orientation towards sustainable product strategies began comparatively late. In the Helsinki Resolution of 1993, sustainable forest management is defined as: "The management and use of forests in a way and at a rate that ensures their biological diversity, productivity, regeneration capacity, vitality and their ability to fulfil relevant ecological, economic and social functions, now and in the future, at local, national and global levels, without causing damage to other ecosystems". (Helsinki Resolution H1 1993) The foundation of the Forest Stewardship Council, FSC for short, at the beginning of the 1990s in response to the environmental policy decisions of the Rio Conference on the Environment (1992) is considered to have initiated a "green" forestry and, in effect, furniture industry. The FSC is an international non-profit organization that developed the first system for certifying sustainable forestry. In the years that followed, other, in some cases competing, certification companies were established. The overarching goal is to manage as large a proportion of forestry as possible in a controlled and sustainable manner. Within a few years of its foundation, the issue of protecting the (rain) forests and the indigenous population became known to the public in the West. In response to a sensitised public, more and more suppliers of wooden furniture and DIY chains switched to developing certified products. For example, the share of environmentally certified furniture in the Otto Group range in 2017 was approximately 54% (Otto Group 2018)—an outstandingly high figure.

Valid figures on the total share of sustainable furniture do not exist. The topic of sustainably produced furniture is present, but de facto hardly plays a role in furniture stores. To date, there is no binding obligation on the part of the manufacturer to prove the source of the raw materials. Likewise, there is no legally binding definition for the sustainable production of furniture—and this despite the fact that the furniture market comprised a sales volume of approximately €34 billion in 2018.

The pioneer of the green furniture industry is the Austrian company "Grüne Erde", which was founded in 1983 by Karl Kammerhofer. As a politically committed bookseller, he had a 5000 address strong customer file of alternative-ecological orientation. By chance he came up with a product idea and developed a natural mattress under the name "Weiße Wolke" (cf. Fig. 2.3). Later, furniture, home accessories, cosmetics and fashion were added. Today, the company, which is now managed by Reinhard Kepplinger and Kuno Haas, employs about 400 people and sells mainly self-produced green furniture made of Central European wood in 14 shops and on the Internet. It achieves a total turnover of approx. 40 million €.

The number of "green furniture stores" besides "Grüner Erde" is manageable. The association of organic furniture stores "ÖkoControl" in Germany, Austria and Switzerland comprises about 40 stores that have set themselves the goal of offering design-oriented but pollutant-free and ecologically and socially strictly tested furnishings. One of the first suppliers of organic furniture was the Cologne store Biomöbel Genske, which was founded in 1986 as Germany's first ecologically oriented furniture store and still exists today.

Fig. 2.3 "Green" white cloud—original product of today's most important eco-furniture manufacturer "Grüne Erde" from Austria. (Courtesy of © Reasons Earth GmbH 2016. All Rights Reserved)

The so-called building biology, which was founded by the physician Hubert Palm and his book "Das gesunde Haus" (The healthy house) (1975), is considered the precursor of green building. The main focus here is on the avoidance of materials that are harmful to health and the recyclability of building materials. A concrete implementation of ecology in construction can already be traced back to the 1970s: At the end of the 1970s, the Baufritz company switched to organic construction methods, avoided chemical building materials, and sourced building materials from certified sources. To this day, Baufritz sets the standards in the field of ecological construction and was awarded the German Sustainability Award for this reason.

The consideration of constructionally evoked energy savings is an outstanding topic of the ecologically oriented construction industry and is also regulated by building law in order to achieve the global climate goals. Today, there is a multitude of networks that address the topic of "green building". In Austria, the forester and entrepreneur Erwin Thoma set high standards for "healthy houses" with his wooden houses, whether private accommodation, government buildings, hotels or residential complexes.

Politically, "green building" becomes attractive as an investment due to lucrative conditions: A green building refers to a building that has been developed and constructed with sustainability in mind. A green building uses resources such as energy, water and materials efficiently and also reduces harmful effects on health and the environment. Sustainability is considered throughout all phases of the building life cycle, from design and construction to operation, maintenance and disassembly. Certification is becoming increasingly relevant, both for occupants and investors. Around 14% (580,000 m^2) of the total take-up in 2018 in the seven largest German cities were certified office buildings.

2.5.3   Tourism

The "Green Hospitality Market" is complex and hardly transparent: lacking definitions, which service elements characterise Green Hospitality, lead to the fact that many providers postulate "green holidays", but a uniform characteristic is not recognisable. Green hospitality can mean the organic breakfast buffet (Motel One) or a comprehensive green holiday concept from the hotel in wooden construction, regenerative energy supply, eco-fair food and integration of social commitment on site (e.g. Selina Hotels with communal beach cleaning of the travellers). Currently, there are about 140 seals or certificates in the field of sustainability in the travel industry. The topic of "green tourism" is booming. In a study by the German Federal Ministry for the Environment, Nature Conservation and Nuclear safety, 57% of respondents said that holidays should be as socially, environmentally and resource-friendly as possible. However, only 4% stated that these factors were decisive when planning a specific holiday (Schmücker et al. 2019).

The market has already responded to the demand side's interest in sustainable travel with corresponding offers. Thus, there are already some sustainable organic hotels in Germany and across Europe that meet people's pronounced interest in sustainability. Their number is not clear. As already described above, the problem of the "label jungle" applies: Due to the high number of different, undefined sustainability certifications, it cannot be clearly determined how many sustainable hotels currently exist (see Table 2.1).

Among the already existing sustainability hotels, a distinction can be made between small establishments and larger chains. It is noticeable that especially the smaller hotels focus on regionality: Organic products from the region, etc. The larger hotel chains use sustainability in particular primarily as a communication tool to improve their image and play on the topic of sustainability selectively and visibly: For example, the Scandic Group emphasises the purchase of 100% green electricity, soap dispensing in refillable dispensers, the reduction of total waste through recycling. Many of the measures save costs for the hotel at the same time. Thus, the sustainability argument is also often used as a waiver argument for guests and employees, such as the two-day room cleaning, missing garbage bags or paperless offices.

Table 2.1   Sustainability in the hotel industry

Hotels with sustainability model	Hotels with sustainable elements
Focus: regionality and use of natural, environmentally friendly materials	Focus: Sustainability as a communication tool
Sustainability is lived "inwardly"	Sustainability is lived "outwardly" (mostly only sustainable facade)
Cooperation with regional partners, food from the direct region	Vintage wood furniture
Most of the hotels are built of wood and natural materials (also from the region).	Conventional construction (mainly concrete)

The results of the German Research Association for Holidays and Travel e. V. (FUR) for 2019, as well as a study by the Leuphana University of Lüneburg, underline the fact that Germans are not as sustainable as they like to claim: According to the study, 71% of German travellers say they are very interested in sustainable travel offers. However, according to the analyses of the actual bookings, only about 33% actually take sustainable aspects into account, for example climate-friendly travel, the selection of ecologically oriented hotels and the avoidance of mass tourism destinations. This behaviour can also be seen in the flight behaviour of Germans. The number of air travels in Germany has increased since the founding of the Fridays for Future movement, as a special analysis of the Federal Statistical Office has shown (Der Spiegel 2019).

2.5.4 Finances

Banks go green: The world's first bank to combine social, ecological and economic criteria, the "Gemeinschaftsbank für Leihen und Schenken", the GLS Bank, was founded in Bochum in 1974 (cf. Fig. 2.4). The lawyer and anthroposophist Ernst Barkhoff developed financing models for free schools, promoted biodynamic agriculture and institutions for people with disabilities. Under the motto "Money is a social means of shaping society if we make it so together", the cooperatively organised bank begins its work and, among other things, invests money in wind power plants at an early stage. In 1991, GLS launches its first wind turbine fund. In 2019, it has more than 242,000 customers (2014: 130,000 customers) in a highly competitive market.

It was not until 2009 that another green bank, the Dutch Triodos Bank, placed its offering in Germany. Umweltbank and Ethikbank followed on a smaller scale. According to the Sustainable Business Institute (SBI), there are currently 380 to 400 sustainability funds in German-speaking countries. According to the Forum Nachhaltige Geldanlage (FNG), the value of all sustainable funds, customer and proprietary investments in Germany was €127.3 billion (enorm 06/2015/16, p. 89 f.).

Fig. 2.4 Original logo GLS Bank. (Courtesy of © GLS Gemmeinschaftsbank eG 2016. All Rights Reserved)

According to a 2016 study by the Bertelsmann Foundation, the volume of investments in financial products that promise investors positive social or ecological effects in addition to a return amounted to €70 million (Petrick and Birnbaum 2016). While the amount invested has tripled since 2012, this means that only 0.3% of the total volume of investment funds used is considered "ethically oriented". In 2014, €15.6 billion was invested in sustainable interest securities, which is about €4.2 billion more than the investment for comparable eco-shares (Heintze 2015/2016, p. 87). In addition, numerous banks are at least slowly changing the rules of profit maximization that were once considered "natural": In addition to the DZ Bank, the Volks- and Raiffeisenbanken, for example, the savings bank subsidiary Deka and some Landesbanken refrain from speculating on the price development of corn, wheat or rice (Heintze 2013, p. 30).

Commerzbank: The "Green" Among the "Giants"
Commerzbank has not made any such investments since 2011 and is considered a "green bank" among the giants thanks to its support for renewable energy. The financial news service Bloomberg included Commerzbank in its list of the world's 20 greenest banks. Since 2011, a so-called "sustainability filter" based on UN criteria has ensured that all investments not only make economic sense, but also achieve a minimum level of sustainability. In addition, however, Commerzbank continues to conduct conventional banking business. Against this backdrop, committed NGOs describe Commerzbank as an ethical pacesetter for banks attempting a sustainable transformation. The environmental organisation Urgewald, which critically observes German economic and export policy, states: "Among the black sheep, the bank is a grey one." (Heintze 2013, p. 33).

In order to establish uniform criteria for sustainability assessment in the financial sector as well, a seal was created in 2016: The so-called FNG seal, initiated by the Forum nachhaltige Geldanlage (Forum for sustainable investments) is an association of 160 banks, investment companies, insurance companies, rating agencies, investment companies and NGOs. It acts as an overarching label for ethical and ecological investment funds.

2.5.5 Consumer Goods

In the FMCG (fast moving consumer goods) sector, there was an increase in new start-ups from the mid-1980s onwards: The environmental mail order company "waschbär" began in 1987 with the so-called "Ökoputzkiste" (Ecocleaningbox) (cf. Fig. 2.5)—it contained nine environmentally friendly cleaning products. Today, the Freiburg-based company offers more than 7000 articles from a wide range of segments. Germany's first phosphate-free cleaning agent was launched in

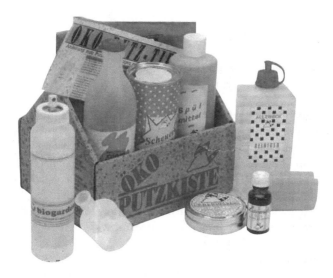

Fig. 2.5 The raccoon's "eco-cleaning box" from 1987. (Courtesy of © Triaz GmbH 2016. All Rights Reserved)

1986 with the Frosch brand of the Mainz-based chemical company Werner&Mertz, which was founded in 1867. In the 1990s, Frosch became the market leader in household cleaning agents—without any advertising. The company's principle: every new product must be the most sustainable within its segment. Three years after the brand launch, Frosch had ecological competition in the form of the Belgian company Ecover, which had already been founded in 1980. Faced with increasing competition and the loss of its top position, Frosch reacted in 2000 with extensive advertising and returned to the top.

Green cosmetics, which emerged almost at the same time as the first consumer-oriented foods, today comprise a total volume of around € 920 million, with almost double-digit growth year after year. Besides brand icons such as Weleda and Dr. Hauschka, about 40 suppliers share the market. Recently, once very small, ambitious companies in this field, such as Lagona Naturkosmetik, have been taken over by large corporations (in this case L'Oreal). The first natural cosmetic products had to be imported from England and France in the 1970s. Lagona itself started with shampoos with an all-natural preservation system. One thing is clear: the understanding of what exactly natural cosmetics are remains highly diverse, if not controversial, to this day.

The Bavarian company memo was founded in 1989 under the commitment of Jürgen Schmidt, who already sold notebooks made of "environmental protection paper" as a schoolboy. The idea: a mail-order business for commercial customers with a complete range of environmentally friendly office supplies and stationery that is no more expensive than conventional products. In the years that followed, the brand expanded its range to include office furniture and promotional materials, and today this portfolio makes it a full-fledged competitor to classic office supplies mail-order companies.

▶ **Conclusion**

If we look at the historical development of the green market, it becomes clear that the individual segments have developed in succession. It is obvious that daily consumption, i.e. food first, has become the focus of a "better" lifestyle: Food is particularly close to us.

It is not without reason that the highest proportion of "organic" certifications is to be found in the area of baby and infant food. One of the best-known organic brands among the general public, HIPP, began farming close to nature as early as the 1950s—today all of the company's products are certified organic (cf. Fig. 2.6).

From this consumption experience in the baby and toddler sector, the desire to make ever more segments of life "greener" developed within the "green" target group sensitized in this way. Pioneers in all areas were mostly micro-initiatives with specific product and service offerings, which eventually became economically viable in niche markets and professionalized and spread with increasing economic success. The Swiss juice manufacturer Biotta switched to organic farming as early as 1951 and has been offering an organic carrot juice since 1957—long before there were any forms of certification. The origins of the natural food juice producer Voelkel even go back to 1936: Karl and Margret Voelkel initially planted apple, pear and cherry trees as well as strawberries, currant and gooseberry bushes in their orchard on the Höhbeck, a sparsely populated stretch of land on the river Elbe in Lower Saxony, and farmed it according to anthroposophical principles. Neither had any knowledge of farming—originally they were a teacher and a sailor. In the 1930s Karl Voelkel drove overland in a three-wheeled small lorry and sold bottled apple juice. After the war, the apple cidery was further professionalized and the juice bottles were sold to health food stores in Hamburg. Already in the 1970s the juices were certified according to the guidelines of the Demeterbund.

The deeply green company Rapunzel from Legau also emerged from a small-scale project: In the autumn of 1974, Joseph Wilhelm and Jennifer Vermeulen founded a self-sufficient community on a farm with a small health food shop in Augsburg, Bavaria. The idea: to produce controlled organic, natural and vegetarian food. Already in 1977, five different products were offered: Muesli, Nutmeal, Gomasio, Treats and Meth. At an early stage, the company focused on the initiation of organic farming. Today the company employs more than 400 people.

The spread of green forms of consumption has also become interesting for large companies: precisely because in highly differentiated and highly competitive displacement markets in terms of marketing, large companies are looking for distinguishing features in order to sharpen their positioning and serve customers even more individually, there is subsequently a cautious adoption of "green products" in the ranges of classic large distribution channels. In the process, three trends are mutually reinforcing:

Fig. 2.6 "Bio-themed" in advertising for the first time—HIPP advertising, 1989. (Courtesy of © HIPP-Werk Georg Hipp OHG 2016. All Rights Reserved)

1. On the one hand, ecological initiatives are present in the media through a permanent thematization of green challenges. The political debate on questions of ecology as well as the exposure of numerous reprehensible conditions in the countries of production make the devastating effects of "cheap consumption" clear and concrete for the end consumer: looking the other way becomes more difficult.

2. More and more people demand from suppliers (at the personal intention level) that they offer ecologically and socially correctly produced goods. If a company does not observe this collectively desired requirement, there will be a breach of trust in the long term, which cannot even be neutralised by consistent performance. In an age in which every consumer can share his or her experiences and assessments with others in real time via the Internet, a failure to enforce ecological-social standards can quickly lead to spreading waves of indignation. Furthermore, the communicative focus on "green example segments" (without any far-reaching economic significance for the company) offers the opportunity to continue the classic segments as before.

3. Highly competitive displacement markets require—as can be read again and again in classical business management theory—the adaptation to changed customer habits and the consideration of apparently increasingly individualized or differentiated target groups. The motto that is wrong in terms of brand sociology, because it replaces brand value, applies: To each customer his product! Irrespective of this, green products continue to offer large companies high differentiation potential—and with better margins than in conventional business.

Summary

The following is the result of the analysis of the green consumption zone:

- Starting with green foods, a sustainable consumption orientation spread to other market segments from the 1980s onwards.
- The consumer sector of ecologically and socially fair fashion becomes a niche market at the end of the 1990s. The ideological shift takes place here, initially among large companies, but then primarily among small and micro businesses and committed fashion designers.
- It was only at the beginning of the 2000s that this development was (re)-recognised by large textile chains, which converted parts of their product ranges to sustainability and entered into voluntary commitments.
- Due to the high degree of anonymity in the textile sector, which in contrast to regional foodstuffs hardly allows any verification, neutral test seals were developed and enforced around the year 2000 to prove the trustworthiness of the goods.
- Almost all consumer sectors are following suit: Even primarily non-green brands are expanding their range to include special green products.

- Many of the organic retailers that are still successful today are characterised by the fact that they started with a "founding product" (i.e. as direct selling manufacturers) and expanded their range with additional products on the basis of their customers. The actual brand strength of many of the early players lies in close networking with their customers, who were prepared to extend their good experiences with "their" supplier to other product areas.

2.6   The Famous Lohas: A Brilliant Marketing Idea

Green branding has evolved from an avant-garde movement to the mainstream. A 2014 study by Saarland University at the Institute for Trade & International Marketing in Germany reveals that 72% of all companies consider the importance of sustainability to be "rather high to very high". Looking ahead, the 54 companies surveyed assume that the topic of sustainability will be relevant for 93% of all companies. In a survey, it was noted that while a good "price-performance ratio" is important for many brand buyers (72%), the criterion "the brand is developing in an environmentally friendly way" is still important for 58% (Zentes 2014, p. 14).

An all-encompassing green lifestyle is indeed possible today. All segments of consumption are covered by "green" offers. An outstanding development, considering the short time span for realization. The reasons certainly lie on the one hand in the business opportunities of the committed companies, but social changes are also driving new forms of economic activity: The meaningfulness of work and one's own actions is important for more and more young decision-makers when choosing a professional activity. Thus, it is precisely young graduates who are willing to perform who form the pioneers within the green industry. Crowdfunding projects not only have a high degree of innovation, but often develop green products in a highly professional manner.

The media and publicity responses to green small businesses are enormous and make it clear which fundamental needs can be satisfied by a well thought-out concept. The publicity impact of the (persuasive) campaigns developed in such projects is always outstanding. Equipped with fractions of the funds that large companies have at their disposal to communicate their concepts, many green pioneers succeed not only in drawing the public's attention to their ideas and products, but also in convincing it to such an extent that projects are pre(!) financed. Interestingly, the communication of these small providers does not get lost in diffuse feel-good images and abstract labels, but they often work in an extremely concrete and detail-oriented way. Even the founders and employees on site have to play a prominent role in order to convince. There is no money available for abstract (advertising) gimmicks, as is still common in the current corporate world, in a self-financed small business that does not have large reserves or financiers. It's no wonder that both product, story and brand, when successful, are often shamelessly copied by larger operations, as has happened with smoothie drinks, where large corporations have adopted the casual, individual style of small suppliers: Innocent, the green pioneer among smoothie companies, was founded in 1998 by three students in England and soon achieved high profile for its unconventional advertising methods (and good taste). As a result, in 2013 the Coca-Cola group bought 90% of the shares. When the then-celebrated Bionade was sold in Germany to the Radeburger-Oetker Group, this led to a failure to redeem the brand values that had ensured its success. A drastic price increase and a wrong advertising and communication policy led to a fundamental drop in sales within a very short time. In the meantime, Bionade belongs to the medium-sized Hassia Group and pursues authentic organic marketing.

The idea of changing framework conditions and expectations also requires a differentiated customer image. In marketing circles, the relevant customer groups of green consumption are summarized under the term "Lohas". For a good 20 years now, the Lohas have been haunting not only the marketing floors, but also lifestyle magazines and various lecture stages. They are regarded as synonymous with a new consumption philosophy and as pioneers for a consumption that confronts companies with new desires, but at the same time promises new lucrative sales markets—especially in times of ever decreasing revenues and structurally perceived product interchangeability. The Loha often seems to be the dream customer of numerous companies that pretend to be innovative. This leads to the paradox that the customer is now the proof of performance and advertising medium of the brand, which is referred to with pride. The question remains: Are the Lohas a trendy ghost or a real strategic basis?

Who or What Are Lohas?

Lohas are people who cultivate a "lifestyle o f health and sustainability". In contrast to the eco-pioneers of the first hour, who mostly satirized their robust grain muesli as long-haired hippies with woolen sweaters, this is a population stratum that wants to enjoy the amenities of economic success in a hedonistic way, but at the same time orient their consumption towards health and sustainability. However, the analysis makes the immediate difficulty clear: what exactly can be understood by sustainability in combination with comfort varies from individual to individual.

The term emerged around 2000 as a zeitgeisty social trend in the USA. Trend experts see the geographical origin of this movement in California. Ever since the emergence of the ecology movement in the 1970s, people there had been open to "green ideas"; people came together who were not averse to the "beautiful life" but nevertheless wanted to distance themselves from pure profit orientation. An individual state that one has to be able to afford and that is therefore typical of post-materialistic structures of a highly differentiated society.

> The increase in social structures that provide physical and psychological security leads to an individualisation of people. Cultural and social needs and motivations become more important. (Cf. Inglehart 1998).

Communications expert Christiane Köhn-Ladenburger believes that world-famous Hollywood stars are directly linked to the successful implementation of the Loha lifestyle: "Attitudes towards products and the companies behind them have changed, and although Hollywood's Lohas do not renounce glitz and glamour, they nevertheless serve as role models and encourage far more people to rethink than demonstrations and resistance manage to do. Fashion, handbags and shoes are still a 'must have' for the stars, and so some well-known labels and designers followed the eco-trend and produce environmentally conscious and ethically correct. Not only material plays a role, but so do working conditions in low-wage countries." (Köhn-Ladenburger 2013, p. 7). The fact that Leonardo di Caprio combined the acceptance of his first Oscar with a plea for the protection of the earth is thus in the good (self-marketing) tradition of the industry.

Consumer researchers are trying to fathom the "essence" of the Lohas more precisely by means of surveys and in-depth psychological interviews. In the process, it is established that the typical lifestyle of Lohas is made up of five megatrends.

Five Megatrends Characterize the Lifestyle of Lohas
1. **Individualisation,** i.e. a (supposedly) independently chosen consumption which is primarily oriented towards personal preferences and views and reviews traditional consumption habits in favour of one's own aesthetic judgement.
2. A **change in values,** i.e. industrialisation (supposedly) frees the individual from social norms and collective expectations. After phases of a hedonistic realization of life, of always more, people today tend to strive to consume less, but better.
3. **New work,** i.e. work is no longer seen merely as a means to an end, but must be meaningful and contribute to self-realization. Attention is paid to a balanced relationship between work and leisure time.
4. **Neo-ecology,** i.e. consumption is no longer thought of only in the here-and-now, but is considered in its global and time-delayed effects on future generations.
5. **Spirituality,** the preoccupation with questions of the meaning of life on a large and small scale. Phases of self-knowledge alternate with everyday life.

According to trend researchers, these five megatrends are the crucial components of the Loha lifestyle. In terms of brand sociology, trends are viewed extremely critically, the descriptions of trends are mostly highly open to interpretation, so that much that is supposed to provide decision-making support and long-term orientation remains unclear. The question is whether trends can be a serious basis for brand work? This will be answered in the following pages. There is no doubt that the relevance for a "green" lifestyle has developed fundamentally in the last 20 years. Many products that were carelessly consumed in the 1980s now have to meet completely different standards—across society—and would fail any food inspection. And yet the question remains, has the consuming individual changed fundamentally? Perhaps "green products" refer to universal core values that have always been ideal-typical objectives, but have now increasingly shifted into the realm of consumption. Isn't the idea of purity, naturalness and honesty something that was already significant in other contexts and has found a home in commodity markets with the increasing disappearance of social structures?

2.7   Are There Green Trends?

Today, innovations are realized in one key term: trend. Trend has long since ceased to be understood in the sense of its original use in the field of fashion and design. In the business world in particular, trends are regarded as possible initiation points for innovations, as blueprints on which new achievements can be established. For trends are characterized in this logic—and this is the decisive differentiating factor from innovation—per se by the fact that they are marketable. The first exploiters are usually the media. In short:

> Trends are only trends when you can sell them. Therefore: Lohas would not have become a serious topic if it had not turned out that this changed consumer demand would represent a lucrative market.

Trends, if they want to be noticed, have to get out of their niche and become relevant to as many people as possible (with high margins). It doesn't matter whether it's new stove tops or an ecological cleaning product.

It is common to think of anything that is "trendy" as synonymous with "cool". This is a rudiment of the enforcement of the term in the context of the fashion world in the early 1990s. Empirically, the only thing that can be established is that "cool" sells ... because something that is cool refers to constantly evolving, being new and surprising. This is the causal link between trend and coolness—it explains the 20-year rise of a term that went from a lifestyle to an economic factor with associated service providers and written material. After all, modern man needs companies that anticipate his needs and thus offer him some peace of mind and reassurance in times of uncertainty or change. Hilariously, the trend itself is subject to speed: The relevance of a specific trend gets shorter every year. For 2019 alone, trend experts diagnosed over 7000 microtrends ... the shelves are filled.

There is therefore no such thing as *a* trend, but rather different manifestations of "cool" forms of change that occur with different effects, i.e. on different social scales: The differentiation into micro-, macro- and megatrends has proven to be expedient. Trend researcher Delia Dumitrescu therefore makes it clear that the question of what is a micro- or a macro-trend can only be explained in terms of its manifestation as an individual example or as a social phenomenon (Dumitrescu 2011, p. 22 ff.). Accordingly, microtrends are small swings, so-called weak signals, which can be identified in concrete products or services. In line with trend theory, small groups of innovative trendsetters are considered to be "weak signal" givers who deviate from classic, enforced behaviour in a certain area in an uncoordinated manner. In most cases, these are initially singular events or short-term phenomena, e.g. new products at trade fairs. If these phenomena evoke resonance, if the new phenomenon spreads and thus becomes permanent, innovation researchers speak of a trend. Finnish futurologist Elina Hiltunen writes: "The truth is, however, that the big changes are already common knowledge. It is the innovations and the events that bring fresh insights and, at best, create a competitive edge." (Dumitrescu 2011, p. 42). Trend is a process of social change. If these signals become visible on a broad scale, i.e. if an actual structural change occurs, trend research speaks of "megatrends". They encompass long-lasting movements of change in social systems.

Megatrends span decades and affect political and social changes. With regard to the megatrend green, this means in concrete terms: light bulbs are banned, organic meals are part of the good manners in every kindergarten, nuclear power is being abolished, bicycle stations are part of election programmes. Being green has become an integral part of everyday culture. For example, "environmental protection" has been a comprehensive topic in Germany for 30 years, constantly involving new aspects (dying forests, nuclear power, rising water levels, etc.), but fundamentally playing an important role on the social agenda.

2.7.1   Brand Sociological Critique of Trend Affinity

Even today, roast pork with brown hunter's sauce is the Germans' favourite meal—despite concerns (and knowledge) about figure, fat values and all the appeals of countless critical consumer protectionists. The proportion of people who order their butter, milk and sausage home via the modern communications medium of the "Internet" is 0.5%, despite the fact that it is so convenient to have your shopping brought to you by supermarkt.de (watch out: bankrupt after 6 months of existence). The rather staid discounter ALDI, whose strongest innovation was the introduction of the scanner checkout in 2002, has been named by far the most trustworthy provider in 2012. It is not the healthy vital bread that sells best, but the modestly "floured grey bread" with crust.

Hardly any other area is as important to the German as his car. It is seen as a way of "taking one's self for a drive" in the truest sense of the word. One would think that this is where individuality is lived in its purest form. The statistics prove otherwise: 77% of all cars are either black, silver or white—with an increasing trend (cf. Kraftfahrtbundesamt 2020). Undercooled designer furniture from Scandinavia or Italy has not managed to become real mass products. The living room cabinet that no longer appears in any hip living magazine may have changed—certainly it is hardly made of rosewood (the forests have already been cleared), but from responsible pine plantation cultivation. The show "Dinner for One" has dream ratings, despite or perhaps because you know exactly what's going to happen. And just before dinner at Christmas, we all still gather around the tree and sing or flute ancient carols. 95.3% of all people state "watching TV" as their favourite leisure activity (cf. Statista 2020b). Men and women today are quota and emancipated, yet only 36%

of all women think it is okay if their partner earns less money than they do. And 90% of all men say they have never left work "because of the children" (only 2.7% of all men took parental leave in 2018). 45% of parents surveyed say they think it's best if the man works full-time and the woman takes care of most of the household along with a part-time job. Even if it seems different to us after watching a football match or a pseudo-documentary series (term: "reality soap opera") on a private channel: just 24% of all Germans have a tattoo (see Statista 2017). Which status symbols do Germans dream of? First place: television—of the latest generation. Second place: a high-class car. Third place: their own holiday apartment or holiday home (for women, the "walk-in wardrobe" is in third place) (cf. Sack et al. 2020).

Cliché? No, statistically verified reality in times of non-stop enlightenment and all-encompassing educational opportunities. It seems hard to portray, but maybe people don't change at all. Maybe many people continue to feel very comfortable doing everything like everyone else. Even someone who likes to be called a "trend guru" takes a very unexcited view of the sameness of life. Scientist Matthias Horx said in a lecture: "We can only ever imagine the future as an apocalypse, a consumer hell or an absurd comic strip. But once we get there, it will turn out to be a perfectly normal place to love, marry, drive a car, and have children."

2.7.2   Media Theme Change

It seems that, on closer inspection, little is changing in people's behaviour and especially in their habits. The founder of German sociology, Ferdinand Tönnies, summarized the connection between habit and well-being in the following triad: Pleasure, habit, memory. Everything we consider beautiful may spring from our "aesthetic judgment"-we cannot be commanded to have a favorite color-but much of what we care about is very often based, solely, on the fact that we have known it over long periods of time. To put it sensitively: At some point, you love your wife/ husband simply because she/he has been around for so long. Without this under-standing, it's hard to see why—structurally speaking—very little changes. No sane person dreams of constant information updates or prefers an online store to a New York shopping tour. As philosopher Renata Saleci puts it under the heading "tyranny of choice": "Today we believe we can choose everything: Who we love, how we look, even the choice of coffee wants to be well thought out. [...] Then there's always the feeling that something even better is waiting around the next corner. So we are never really satisfied. And are reluctant to settle." (Schultz 2013) What does this mean for the brand?

Symbolic violence—roughly summarised as orientation towards the existing—as the French sociologist Pierre Bourdieu called it, is profoundly human and locates us in a complex and increasingly hectic environment. Sociologically, the more accelerated the world, the more conservative our decisions. The more confused the world around us, the more important it is to have stable structures. Hardly anyone likes living alone and being confronted with something new every hour. New things may fascinate for a limited time, but "the best part is coming home." Motorhomes (more than 530,000 vehicles in Germany in 2019) are also becoming more numerous because, like a snail shell, they piggyback one's own room, one's own retreat, on long journeys—especially when the world is becoming increasingly confusing.

The real achievement of the trend drivers is to magnify minority behaviour immeasurably. This is what the media thrives on—yesterday's newspaper is known to wrap fish in. Minority behaviour becomes mainstream and mainstream becomes the crude crankery of absolute recluses, or so it seems. The opposite is true: what no one writes about is the real world. Exactly there, where everything is known, life takes place. It is only unfortunately media-uninteresting, because it already exists and does not arouse any needs—it does not sell more than anyway. It is the bread-and-butter of consumerism. Trend researchers know that this is the case. So is it much more about the assertiveness of trends? The famous one-percenters who would change the world? If it were so, there would be constant and permanent upheavals and innovations—this is also not the case. Because:

> Trends only have a chance of really catching on and becoming mass-market if they appear as familiar as possible. In short: every innovation should be denovated as quickly as possible.

A principle that is known from musicology. Because only those songs have mass potential that sound as if one had already heard them at some point … the masses seek out the familiar, because man is evolutionarily polarized in such a way that he always chooses the familiar—only in this way could survival be ensured in primeval times. In concert, the real pleasure begins when the band starts to play their well-known songs: Songs that are already socially charged to the brim with the audience's personal memories. The brand owes its existence to this deeply human behavior.

2.7.3 Acceleration as Actual Content

A topsy-turvy world. If you believe the media, advertising and trend experts, no stone is left unturned in the modern world. This phenomenon is best explained by the fact that here, too, the demand for acceleration is increasingly displacing the value of information. Today, it is not the statement as such that plays the decisive role, but the speed of information. Precisely because novelty has the highest value in an information society, it displaces the actual content.

If one understands brands as social phenomena that have business implications, it becomes clear that the trending topic of "green branding" is either part of a company's ingrained genetics—or not. It is often believed that a company can "just jump" on the eco *zeitgeist* thanks to marketing that conjures up an ideal green advertising world, shows off some green activities or cobbles together some sustainable attributes from the miracle box of advertising art (right down to its own eco seals). Reality proves: In the long run, only what is actually delivered on the performance level can develop resonance. For example, it is now repeatedly marketing fashion to ask potential customers what they want from a brand, or even overarching social contexts, especially via social media: Ford asked the question of what is "typically German" in order to adapt its brand based on the results. These pseudo-participatory elements are highly questionable as they are not serious attempts at dialogue: In reality, the advertising responses lie ready-made in the drawer of the client and agency and are published in a carefully planned manner.

Against this background, a trend-oriented marketing strategy is of no use at all if it does not first focus on the real performance level of the company and is geared towards an *actual* dialogue. McDonald's can color its logo even greener, add more meatless salads to the menu, and offer even more vegan burgers: The day is far off when McDonald's becomes the preferred hangout of hungry vegans—and that scenario shouldn't be management's desired goal. On the contrary: brand thrives on differentiation, even in the face of trends. Our question is: What would actually happen if a McDonald's were simply a McDonald's again?

The methodology to work out this anchored success structure of a company is presented in Chap. 3 ("Understanding the brand"). The goal is to understand the brand as a social system in its closely networked interrelationships. Instead of working on the surface, it is necessary to work out in a scientifically well-founded way which individual cause-effect relationships exist in a brand and how the brand functions as an alliance system. The following questions are in the foreground:

- What actually is a brand?
- What internal forces are at work within it?
- Why do people choose certain brands and why not?
- What conditions individual and social trust?
- What makes strong brands strong?

Only when the collective dynamics of brand sociology are known can the available findings be used in a targeted manner in the sense of "green brand management". Brand sociology borrows its scientific basis from the knowledge of the constant behavioural and structural formation patterns of individual people, but above all of human togetherness. Social laws that are just as valid in the age of social media and virtual networks as they were hundreds of years ago, when networks were still real-social. Human beings and their individual and social needs have not changed significantly in structural terms. Analogously, the success patterns of strong brands demonstrate an incredible ability to develop social pull. In the case of prominent brands such as Apple or, in the green sector, Weleda, they even manage to turn people into "disciples" of the brand to some extent. People who spare no expense and effort for "their" brand and, in the case of Apple, sometimes squat down on the asphalt for a night with a blanket in order to be the first to purchase a new electronic device the next morning.

From a purely analytical point of view, all successful brands have strong similarities within their success structures—regardless of whether they sell hip electronic devices, a service or organic food. These structures and their disclosure are what we want to focus on. The sociological perspective enables a view of brands that makes one thing clear above all:

> A brand is just as controllable as sales, controlling or product development.

A look at brand reality makes it clear that this fact is not taken into account by most brand managers: Brand is seen as an attractive fascination that optionally has something to do with awareness, symbolism, advertising, myth, psychology or emotion (in the worst case combined with the self-actualization of a senior manager). To anticipate at this point: These classifications are completely superficial, they lead to serious management mistakes every day and do not do justice to the economically decisive facts of the brand.

References

Allensbach Institute for Public Opinion Research (2020) Allensbacher Markt- und Werbeträger-Analyse - AWA 2020. Allensbach

Appinio (2019) Do you pay attention to sustainability when buying clothes? https://de.statista.com/statistik/daten/studie/1133775/umfrage/umfrage-zum-kauf-von-nachhaltiger-kleidung-in-der-dach-region/. Accessed 23 Nov 2020

Bowen H (1953) Social responsibilities of the businessman. Harper, New York

Carroll AB (1979) A three-dimensional conceptual model of corporate performance. Acad Manag Rev 4(4):497–505

Carson R (1987) The silent spring. Beck'sche Reihe, Munich

Commission of the European Communities (2001) Green Paper European framework for corporate social responsibility. http://www.europarl.europa.eu/meetdocs/committees/deve/20020122/com(2001)366_en.pdf. Accessed 30 Oct 2020

Der Spiegel (1994) Auf dem Öko-Trip. Der Spiegel, 14 Nov. 1994. https://www.spiegel.de/spiegel/print/d-13693394.html. Accessed 4 Nov 2020

Der Spiegel (2019) Analysis of air traffic data: more German air passengers - despite "Fridays for Future". https://www.spiegel.de/reise/fernweh/fridays-for-future-mehr-deutsche-flugpassagiere-trotz-klimaprotesten-a-1290638.html. Accessed 23 Nov 2020

Die Zeit (2017) Despite emissions scandal: Volkswagen sells more cars. https://www.zeit.de/news/2017-07/19/auto-vw-konzern-verkauft-im-ersten-halbjahr-mehr-autos-19112802?utm_referrer=https%3A%2F%2F. Accessed 23 Nov 2020

Dumitrescu D (2011) Road trip to innovation. How I came to understand future thinking. TrendOne, Hamburg

Enorm (2015) Statistics on the acceptance of eco-labels. Enorm 02/2015: Hamburg

Faitrade Germany (2019) Faitrade turnover rises to 1.6 billion euros. Faitrade Germany. https://www.fairtrade-deutschland.de/service/presse/details/fairtrade-umsatz-steigt-auf-16-milliarden-3230.html. Accessed 28 Aug 2020

Faller H (2013) Stiftung Warentext: "Rationale Argumente treten bei Kosmetika in den Hintergrund". ZEITmagazin 51/2013. https://www.zeit.de/2013/51/stiftung-warentest-produkttest. Accessed 23 Nov 2020

Federal Environment Agency (2014) Umweltbewusstsein in Deutschland 2014 - Vertiefungsstudie: Umweltbewusstsein und Umweltverhalten junger Menschen, Umweltbundesamt 2016. https://www.umweltbundesamt.de/sites/default/files/medien/376/publikationen/texte_77_2015_umweltbewusstsein_in_deutschland_2014_vertiefungsstudie.pdf. Accessed 30 Oct 2020

Federal Ministry of Food and Agriculture (BMEL) (2020) Germany, as it eats - The BMEL Nutrition Report 2020. https://www.bmel.de/SharedDocs/Downloads/DE/Broschueren/ernaehrungsreport-2020.pdf?__blob=publicationFile&v=21. Accessed 4 Nov 2020

Fromm E (1976) To have or to be. Deutscher Taschenbuch Verlag, Munich

Global Standard nonprofit (2020) Our vision, our mission. https://www.global-standard.org/de/ueber-uns/unsere-vision-unsere-mission.html. Accessed 4 Nov 2020

Grefe C (2016) Good food, poor farmers. Die Zeit 20/2016. https://www.zeit.de/2016/20/produktionsstandard-siegel-zertifikate-einfluss-bauern-entwicklungslaender. Accessed 4 Nov 2020

Grimm F (2014) Design or not to be. Enorm: 05/2014, Hamburg

Hauff V (ed) (1987) Our common future. The Brundtland report of the World Commission on Environment and Development. Eggenkamp Publishing House, Greven

Heintze A (2013) Step by step. Enorm: 05/2013, Hamburg

Heintze A (2015/2016) Investment in Grün. Enormous: 06/2015/16, Hamburg

Henrichs B (2013) There is another way. Enorm 01, Feb/March 2013, Hamburg

Ingelhart R (1998) Modernization and postmodernization. Cultural, economic and political change in 43 societies. Campus Verlag, Frankfurt/Main

Jünger FG (2010) The perfection of technology. Klostermann, Frankfurt/Main

Köhn-Ladenburger C (2013) Marketing for Lohas. Communication concepts for demanding customers. Springer Gabler, Wiesbaden

Köhrer E (2013) The little ones drive the big ones. Interview with Kirsten Brodde. Enorm 05/2013, Hamburg

Kraftfahrtbundesamt (2020) Proportion of colours in newly registered passenger cars (Pkw) in Germany in 2019. https://de.statista.com/statistik/daten/studie/5101/umfrage/anteil-der-farben-an-den-pkw-neuzulassungen/. Accessed 24 Nov 2020

Maase K (1997) Grenzenloses Vergnügen: the rise of mass culture 1850–1970. Fischer Taschenbuch Verlag, Frankfurt/Main

Meadows D, Meadows DH, Zahn E, Milling P (1972) The limits to growth. Report of the Club of Rome on the state of humanity. Rororo, Reinbek near Hamburg

Ministerial Conference on the Protection of Forests in Europe (1993) Helsinki Resolution H1. General guidelines for the sustainable management of forests in Europe. http://www.foresteurope.org/docs/MC/MC_helsinki_resolutionH1.pdf. Accessed 30 Oct 2020

Noelle-Neumann E (1989) The theory of the spiral of silence as an instrument of media effects research. In: Kaase M, Schulz W (eds) Massenkommunikation. Cologne Journal of Sociology and Social Psychology, vol 30. VS Verlag, Wiesbaden

Otto Group (2018) Press Release Otto Group. Pressebox.de 09.05.2018. https://www.pressebox.de/inaktiv/otto-gmbh-co-kg/Otto-Group-baut-nachhaltiges-Mode-und-Moebelsortiment-aus/boxid/905163. Accessed 30 Oct 2020

Palm H (1975) The healthy house, the sick house and its cure. Our next environmentalism. The biological theory of building in the Architectura perennis. In: The civilization diseases of architecture. A recipe book for self action. Ordo-Verlag, Dettingen

Peattie K (1992) Green marketing. Pitman Publishing, London

Petrick S, Birnbaum J (2016) Social impact investing in Deutschland. Marktbericht 2016. Kann das Momentum zum Aufbruch genutzt werden? Bertelsmann-Stiftung

Pufé I (2017) Sustainability. UTB, Constance

Radkau J (2011) The era of ecology. A world history. Beck, Munich

Randers J (2016) 2052. Rhe new report to the Club of Rome: a global forecast for the next 40 years. Oekom, Munich

Sack A, Strohmaier B, Parkin C (2020) How Germans are finally learning to love luxury. Die Welt Oct 26, 2015. http://www.welt.de/icon/article148007519/Wie-die-Deutschen-endlich-lernen-den-Luxus-zu-lieben.html. Accessed 30 Oct 2020

Schmücker D, Sonntag U, Günther W (2019) Sustainable holiday travel: awareness and demand development. Baseline study based on data from the 2019 travel analysis. https://www.bmu.de/fileadmin/Daten_BMU/Pools/Forschungsdatenbank/fkz_um18_16_502_nachhaltigkeit_reiseanalyse_2019_bf.pdf. Accessed 4 Nov 2020

Schultz S (2013) Capitalism is the neurosis of humanity. Interview with Renata Saleci. SpiegelOnline, 24 Jun 2013. http://www.spiegel.de/wirtschaft/service/tyrannei-der-wahl-freiheit-kann-ueberfordern-a-906199.html. Accessed 30 Oct 2020

Serviceplan (2019) Fashion sustainability study. Munich

Statista (2017) Do you have tattoos? https://de.statista.com/statistik/daten/studie/718861/umfrage/umfrage-zum-vorhandensein-von-tattoos-in-deutschland/. Accessed 23 Nov 2020

Statista (2020a) New SUV registrations: every 5th newly registered car is an SUV. https://de.statista.com/infografik/19572/anzahl-der-neuzulassungen-von-suv-in-deutschland/. Accessed 23 Nov 2020

Statista (2020b) Most popular leisure activities, activities and sports (at least several times a month) in Germany from 2016 to 2019. https://de.statista.com/statistik/daten/studie/171601/umfrage/mehrmals-pro-monat-ausgeuebte-freizeitaktivitaeten/. Accessed 24 Nov 2020

Steiner R (2011) Geisteswissenschaftliche Grundlagen zum Gedeihen der Landwirtschaft: Landwirtschaftlicher Kursus. Rudolf Steiner Publishing House, Basel

Winkelmann M (2014/2015) The organic trade is at a crossroads. Interview with Klaus Braun. Enorm 06/2014/2015, Hamburg

Zentes J (ed) (2014) Sustainable brand management. Institute of Retailing & International Marketing (H.I.M.A.) of Saarland University, March 2014

Understanding the Brand

3

Abstract

In order to successfully manage a brand, a sound scientific knowledge of the effective laws and dynamics of brand building and brand strengthening is required. The basic laws of brand management refer to the knowledge of the consistent behavioural patterns of individual people, but above all of human interaction. In this chapter, it is shown that brand is first of all a social phenomenon that has direct economic effects. Against this background, the crucial key concepts and relationships of brand sociology such as self-similarity, trust and energy system are explained and illustrated with many practical examples. It becomes clear that a brand is first and foremost a "positive prejudice", which is capable of lowering transaction costs and reducing the effort of persuasion in advertising and communication.

3.1 A Tricky Thing: The Brand as a Social Alliance System

Brands do not have a good press with enlightened people: Although they promise us wonderfully cared-for skin, perfect driving pleasure or simply a delicious pizza, the rational "consumer" vigorously resists the dictatorship of business enterprises, which do not stop at looking for their victims even in the schoolyard. Canadian physicist and philosopher Ursula Franklin is quoted as saying, "We are occupied just as the French or Norwegians were occupied by the Nazis in World War 2, but now they are whole armies of marketers." (Klein 2000, p. 311). Naomi Klein became a consumerist icon and book millionaire atwo decades ago with her meticulously researched book, No Logo. The idea, carefully cultivated by politics and the associated consumer groups, that man is a "homo oeconomicus" who carefully weighs and compares in order to finally make a sovereign-rational purchase decision, contradicts practical life experience: Hundreds of thousands of gigantic SUVs (sales figures increasing) with high fuel consumption are driving on German roads—

© Springer Fachmedien Wiesbaden GmbH, part of Springer Nature 2022   59
O. Errichiello, A. Zschiesche, *Green Branding*,
https://doi.org/10.1007/978-3-658-36060-3_3

although one could get from A to B just as easily with a dwarf-like vehicle of the Fiat brand. We care for our skin with products "from the blue can" and ask for a "Hamburger", although this pulp costs three times as much as the equally effective but unknown "white" products. Tap water is sometimes healthier than products from thousand-year-old glacier ice springs, and yet there are thousands of mineral water brands in Europe alone. The reality of life proves that people of the post-modern age do not *consume,* rather they selectively choose and decide en masse for a certain branded product despite logical counter-arguments and are pleased (hidden, of course) when they have the well-known premium product instead of the "own brand" on the festively laid table at the birthday party in the family circle. This may be denounced by progressive admonishers and castigated as despicable indoctrination by committed educators, but it doesn't change the fact that brands occupy fields of everyday life and sometimes help guide our actions. A nerve is being struck. It's about a social fact that is worth analyzing in a completely unemotional way.

It is not only in everyday life that people complain about "brand terror"; the scientific debate about brands and advertising is as old and everyday as modern mass-produced goods themselves: Sociologist Werner Sombart wrote in 1908 that brand advertising "shamelessly drags the ugly processes of demand satisfaction into the light and possibly wants to immerse them in beauty." (Sombart 1908, p. 285). Criticism of mass merchandising became mass effective in the late 1950s when American publicist Vance Packard linked the concepts of brand, advertising, and manipulation (Packard 1962). In 1960, Raymond Williams (1961, p. 170 ff.) wrote in his essay "The magic system" that advertising played a key role for the capitalist system and conditioned people. In his analysis "Critique of the Aesthetics of Commodities" (Haug 1971) Wolfgang Haug revealed how it was possible for brands and advertising to rise to prominence. Amir Kassaei, one of Germany's most prominent advertisers, makes a similar polemic: "While the whole world is thinking about sustainability, advertisers are the last to make loud propaganda for unrestrained consumerism. We are the front pigs of a system built on quantitative growth. We try to sell people goods they don't need and educate them to define themselves through consumption." (Schmoll and Winkelmann 2015, p. 69). Ultimately, Kassei retired from the advertising industry for these listed reasons.

In contrast, the social scientist Wolfgang Pohrt sees capitalism and its products, the brand, as a law of culture, as it were: "It is not the rule of people over people, but a factual context rules over people, which has been created by them themselves." (Pohrt 2013, p. 89). He makes clear how independently acting economic actors nevertheless depend on and act with each other. This uncoordinated sequence of actions results in dynamics that are beyond the individual's desire or control. Pohrt writes: "Let us rather look at the facts: since capital has existed, it has stumbled from one crisis to the next. In the process, it thrives magnificently; downfalls act on capital like a fountain of youth. [. . .] The 'second nature', as Marx occasionally called the capital relation, because it confronts people with the power of an alien, inscrutable and untamed force of nature, this 'second nature' is also similar to the first in the sense that every end is a beginning [. . .]." (Pohrt 2012, p. 50 f.). The philosopher

Ralf Konersmann summarizes: Capitalism embodies "evil" that always creates "good" (Konersmann 2015, p. 264).

The topic of brands fascinates and interests. There is hardly a party leader, board member or prelate who does not talk about the brand essence of his party, his company or his church—and nods extremely seriously into the camera. Even a socialist country like East Germany could not do without brands and created performance systems that, as Dr. Quendt, f6, Kathi, Nudossi or pasta from Riesa, have long outlived their country of origin and at least convey a sense of home on the dinner table (Zschiesche and Errichiello 2009). In contrast to a profit-oriented market economy, the dictum of "to each according to his needs" stood in the foreground, true to Marxist social theory. Elaborate styling or advertising was considered synonymous with capitalist methods and a nonsensical cost factor (even if there was a separate, at times downright avant-garde GDR advertising show, the "tausend teletips"/ttt, from 1959 to 1976). Nevertheless, even from the simple packaging and naming, East German population constructed its own brands. Today there is a strong market for these sometimes dearly loved products, which were an important cultural component of a country that had disappeared. Anyone who has ever experienced the atmosphere at the Ostpro trade fair for Eastern products in Berlin, Erfurt or Dresden understands immediately: brands are cultural bodies.

3.1.1 No Goods Market Without Branded Goods

Brand has played a significant role in all societies and since the beginning of commodity markets. The more globalisation takes place, the more important place becomes—even if cosmopolitan managers never tire of propagating exactly the opposite. Places are not only bound to geography, but can become attached to things in the sense of memes, i.e. collective places of memory: The special coffee from Italy that one discovered on vacation, the Playmobil pirate ship that is now handed to one's children in the bathtub (16 million copies sold). People associate certain things with experiences and adventures. Joseph von Eichendorff, not primarily known as a marketer (but he was), wrote, "Sleeps a song in all things." True. Brands, consciously or unconsciously, are a lived, sometimes beloved, piece of everyday culture and thus a social fact summarized by the word "habit." Habits are the "living room of the soul", all the more important that everything is neat and manageable there when the world is constantly reinventing itself and sometimes collapsing with a loud bang. With reference to the anthropologist Marc Augé, the philosopher Alexander Pschera makes the following observation with regard to the formation of social identity: "A non-place is not legible and not describable because it is without reference. Lack of reference, however, creates discomfort. Empty train station halls, bare hotel rooms, backyards, nocturnal supermarket parking lots: These are places of such emptying of meaning through strangeness. In these backdrops of nothingness there is no anchor point. One falls into the bottomless pit of the loneliness of things." (Pschera 2011, p. 54). This makes it all the more important to stand for something as a brand or to vouch for a service.

3.1.2   Karl Marx: The First Brand Theorist

The brand only appears comprehensible and concrete when the mass-effective dynamics of a brand are analysed with the "sociological toolbox". Brand is primarily a social phenomenon that has economic effects—not the other way around. Whether we like it or not, man incessantly composes certain interpretations and worlds of feeling from the subjects surrounding him. All consumer terror? In view of the diverse as well as mass marketing and advertising literature of the present, it seems interesting that a famous philosopher dealt early on with the nature of the brand, whose intellectual "followers" did everything they could to overcome these very brands: Karl Marx. In 1866, in the fourth section of his book on Capital, he wrote: "A commodity seems at first sight a self-evident, trivial thing. Its analysis reveals it to be a very intricate thing, full of metaphysical sophistry and theological quirks. So far as it has use-value, there is nothing mysterious about it, whether I look at it from the point of view that it satisfies human needs by its properties, or receives these properties only as the product of human labor." (Marx 1973, p. 85). A carpenter who makes a table may have produced a commodity from wooden slats, but it is only its sale that gives the table a different essence: "For as soon as it appears as a commodity, it is transformed into a sensuous, supersensuous thing. It not only stands with its feet on the ground, but it turns itself upside down in relation to all other commodities, and develops crickets from its wooden head, much more whimsically than if it began to dance of its own free will." (Marx 1973, p. 85). Marx is downright helpless in describing the nature of the modern product, which not only satisfies need but changes as a commodity by assuming a subject character.

With this analysis, Marx emerges as a decidedly early marketing theorist; many experts today would hardly claim otherwise when it comes to the topic of brand. In a time when all decisions are no longer made because an entrepreneur "believes" in them, but because a manager has evaluated sales and market research figures, the brand is one of the last unknowns. When it comes to brand, not only committed parents and self-proclaimed consumer protectionists become emotional, but also otherwise completely rational company leaders. Brand, we hear again and again, is emotion, lifestyle and value, to name a few typical buzzwords. Such characteristics are much more difficult to measure than business figures. Does this mean that Ferrari is a brand, but not Lidl or the organic food store on the street corner? In order to answer this question and to understand some prejudices, it must first be clarified how and why brands have developed and what brands actually are from a structural point of view.

3.2   Two Thousand Years of Brands and Advertising

Historically, brands are old: In Pompeii, paintings can be found on the walls of houses, wordily inviting people to visit nearby wine taverns. Historians noted that Roman clay jugs of antiquity bore the imprint "sine cera"—without wax. A proof of performance that made it clear to customers that this manufacturer only produced jugs of the very best quality and did not have to conceal any cracks in the vessel with wax—one of the first trademarks. In the Middle Ages, the craft guilds stamped their seal on the manufactured goods in order to praise the "guildiness", i.e. the goods manufactured according to the best craft custom, even outside a geographically limited place of manufacture. And in the early modern period, craftsmen used so-called "trade cards" to draw attention to their special achievements with pictures and text. As a mass phenomenon, trade marks in Germany are closely linked to industrialisation and the granting of freedom of trade at the beginning of the nineteenth century: With increasing urbanization, on the one hand, there was a growing distance between producers of a good and its buyers, and on the other hand, the concentration of potential buyers in a spatially manageable area allowed production to be directed towards the future. In a world where most buyers had no connection with the supplier of their milk or bread, brands were a means of nevertheless publicly anchoring knowledge and an expected performance under a particular name. The health food stores in particular, as a result of the Lebensreform movement in the mid-nineteenth century, which facilitate a lifestyle close to nature and responsible consumption, are an ideal type of this idea.

In a market that is becoming more and more anonymous, it was important to secure trust and to become or remain recognizable. This meant working out its own service specifics. Advertising and design had the task of disseminating information as comprehensively as possible and structuring trust through recognition. The brand therefore presents a reliable offer with the help of advertising. The triumph of the brand and advertising were two aspects that reinforced each other. The more unfamiliar, the more communicative orchestration to make the unfamiliar familiar and thus trustworthy. Or, as the saying goes: you can only ever trust the familiar.

One of the pioneers of branding in Germany today is Karl August Lingner, inventor and CEO of the mouthwash Odol. In 1893, the entrepreneur launched a massive advertising campaign that established brand advertising in Germany—so much so that the brand is still known today, although its advertising presence has declined massively. The fact that the triumphant advance of the branded article started with a mouthwash seems consistent in historical retrospect: the first advertising efforts appeared in the sixteenth century at the margins of the economic system: Due to guild regulations, advertising was only allowed for products that were not subject to any ordinances; these were largely dubious remedies and medicines as well as books.

The stigma that advertising is something dishonest has changed relatively little in global advertising spending, which at one point exceeded the level of some gross domestic products. This makes the advertising industry all the more vigorous in its attempts to cover up its inglorious past in large part by presenting itself as a contemporary art form. Peter Zernisch, an advertiser for over 35 years, wrote the following character portrait of advertising agencies in 2003: "The advertising agencies, originally once space jobbers and advertisement expeditions, have in the course of about a hundred years moulted from declared representatives of the media industry to representatives of communicative creativity. [. . .] Although the creatives in the service of the brand remain anonymous outside the narrowest professional public, their works shine much more visibly than in the markets of the established arts." (Zernisch 2003, p. 73).

The brief historical derivation reveals the structure of brands. Before a brand sociological focus, marked products are initially a system that succeeds in embodying certain performance projections. It does not matter how large or economically significant a company is. From a brand sociological point of view, it is irrelevant whether it is a multinational company or a regional fruit supplier, as long as people associate a name with similar knowledge and in the best case—through the constant fulfilment of positive expectations—trust.

3.2.1   A "Good Name" Is Created When (Pre-)Trust Exists

The German sociologist Niklas Luhmann (2000) describes trust as a state in which we already know the basics, are already informed, even if not completely. By possessing this very knowledge, the degree of complexity of our environment is reduced. Suddenly, from this basic trust in certain things, options for action directed towards the future arise. Otherwise, survival in differentiated societies is not possible. The strong brand as a "condensed meaning" sends clear messages over time and, if managed consistently, receives an increasing amount of trust from its clientele. Brand is an obligatory performance claim that becomes a "good name" when that commitment—and social resonance to its performance—is met. How should a trip to the supermarket in the twenty-first century work without pre-confidence and personal pre-knowledge of some products? The poor person without any positive product pre-experience would die of thirst (or freeze to death) in front of the refrigerated shelf before even deciding on a milk. A Toyota is only looked under the bonnet pro forma, and with a natural yoghurt from Andechser we assume with a high degree of certainty that there is no formaldehyde in it.

It is clear that a "normal" everyday life as a social being in a complex world without a certain pre-confidence in certain things and processes is hardly liveable or representable. Otherwise the human being would be completely incapable of acting. We notice how important a basic trust is for our self-perception and personal classification of the environment when events such as Chernobyl, Fukushima, the Corona crisis, a crime or an unexpected loss of a partner or a job completely shake our "normal" world and thus our consistent view, which until then was considered secure.

Whether a regional pub or a global player: For a company it is true that an externally existing pre-confidence in its own performance makes it possible to act economically, i.e. with foresight. With a certain number of people who have a pre-confidence and regularly purchase the service, purchasing and sales, in short the entire value chain, can be designed. The economist Carl Christian von Weizsäcker therefore describes trust in relation to economic bodies as a "coordination mechanism" between buyer and seller: a socially accelerating mechanism that ensures that transaction costs for the company fall considerably. In return, the customer experiences considerable personal deceleration, because his effort to check, his drive to compare, decreases significantly over time. The enterprise may feel relieved to that extent, because its daily explanation and communication expenditure is minimized. In this context, trust is by no means to be understood as an ethical end in itself, but rather describes a social bonding energy that is monetarily a no-brainer for the company—with sensitive observance of all the rules of maintaining trust in the brand. Von Weizsäcker sums up the value of trust in sociological terms: "The buyer is interested in a certain service, a certain product. Its value to him depends on what characteristics of use it actually has. As a rule, it would be very costly for him to convince himself before buying the service or good by his own inspection that it actually has the characteristics of use desired by him. He can save himself this effort if he trusts the seller to supply him with a service or good that really has the properties he hopes for." (von Weizsäcker 2001, pp. 249–261).

An almost ideal example of how trust considerably facilitates and accelerates everyday life not only with classic "external" customers, but also internally, and also serves quality assurance, is provided by the German organic pioneer in the field of essential oils, founded in 1986: the company Primavera, which from its company location in Oy-Mittelberg in the Allgäu region has built up a worldwide network of now 15 organic cultivation partners, who supply the company with raw materials largely in organic quality. These people, often closely associated with the company for decades, or mostly agricultural cooperatives from Peru to Turkey to Cambodia or Bhutan, supply the company primarily with high-quality natural essential oils. From the more than 90 raw materials supplied, ready-to-use aroma care products are produced from the foot of the Alps and shipped to 32 countries worldwide. The product range includes over 150 individual essential oils, mainly from organic cultivation, as well as aroma care products for use in conjunction with therapy, room fragrancing and natural cosmetics (see Fig. 3.1). The "naturally" grown friendships to the cultivation partners all over the world are the lynchpin of the entrepreneurial success or, as Andrea Dahm, longtime responsible for the area of brand management and sustainability, describes the beginnings:

> In the 1980s, high-quality natural oils were a rarity. Therefore, our founders Ute Leube and Kurt L. Nübling set out on a worldwide search for farmers and essential oil producers who could deliver organic quality and share the vision of their young company. One year after the company was founded, a young farmer from Provence became the first organic cultivation partner. A friendly business relationship that to this day is based solely on mutual trust— there is no contract. To this day, the basis of all our relationships is mutual trust. But this is never given from the beginning. And it is not manifested by signatures on a piece of paper. That was never our intention. Far more important to us and our cultivation partners than any contract is the word. Over the years, we have experienced and learned that our trusting cooperation works when everyone shares the same values—first and foremost, a love of nature, enthusiasm for essential oils and a passion for quality. (Dahm 2021)

The relationship and trust work requires Primavera to meet a variety of demands—on a social as well as on a product level. This means that the company contributes to the costs of production, the pre-financing of plants and seeds, for certification as well as prepayment for harvests, but also provides financial means for

Fig. 3.1 With iconic oil vial on the cultivation field: Andrea Dahm with company founder Kurt L. Nübling and the Purchasing Manager for Raw Materials, Ioanna Mantzouki in India at Primavera's "Eucalyptus Project" (from left to right). (Courtesy of © Primavera Life GmbH 2020. All rights reserved)

the construction of a training center (India) if required. The prices for the essential oils are set in direct consultation with the farmers and are sometimes many times the world market price. Support in creating or maintaining the market and sales promotion are also part of the intensive cooperation. In return for the company's input, the local farmers and distillers use their many years of experience and specialist knowledge to work with the plants in order to be able to supply the best possible quality of oil, free of pesticides, genetic engineering, etc. Thus, the personally trusting relationships with the cultivation partners are a commitment with high benefits for all sides—not least for the customers, who trust that they are buying high-quality natural oils. Founder Kurt L. Nübling accordingly describes trust as "the core of our company's success." (Dahm 2021).

It is all the more devastating when a company abuses this pre-confidence of its customers—because in this case there is a "crisis of confidence" because the expected services have not been provided. Robert Bosch many decades ago said, "I'd rather lose money than trust." He knew—long before there was a word like marketing or brand management—loss of trust is a catastrophe for a brand. Cuba's former Minister of Industry, Che Guevara, put this connection into words as follows: "Quality is respect for the people."

The general distrust in the market, on the other hand, is continuously increasing, describes the magazine Ökomagazin enorm in an editorial with the title "Trust me!"

There it is described that the multitude of regular scandals at banks, insurance companies (e.g. useless products), food manufacturers (e.g. price fixing), the uncovering of inhumane production conditions, tax avoidance models, the widespread label fraud and the most malicious violations of animal welfare with which the public is confronted in the media, have permanently damaged basic trust in manufacturers and service providers. In representative consumer studies on the trustworthiness of companies, negative records are repeatedly broken. Incidentally, the worst performers are regularly energy suppliers, banks and, above all, food manufacturers (cf. enorm 03/2015, p. 19). This is interesting because the food sector in particular is the nucleus of an ecologically trustworthy goods economy (see Sect. 2.3.2). In response to this, it has been observed that more and more people are buying regional products. The knowledge of knowing the producer or at least his region of origin and even being able to check on him personally (in theory) conveys a feeling of security—basically a regression to the beginning of the first commodity markets, when producer and buyer knew each other. It is not without reason that the largest food retail association, EDEKA, stages itself accordingly: they know that size intimidates, stands for anonymity and inaccessibility, and therefore emphasize the regional integration of each individual store, assign a named owner to the store (for example "E aktiv markt Jessen" in Hamburg-Bergstedt) and use the employees working there for communication and advertising. EDEKA does everything it can as a modern "corner shop" to evoke proximity and direct regionality even in the districts of large cities. The fact that some products from the region then receive their own shelf stickers ("From the region") rounds off the picture. No wonder that EDEKA scores above average in the GRPA trust index.

Just how stable social trust is is proven by the results of the population-representative "Readers Digest Most Trusted" study from 2019. For example, Volkswagen continues to be regarded by Germans—despite Dieselgate—as the most trusted company in the automotive industry (see Most Trusted Brands 2019).

The good name of the company is always a context of obligation—especially in "wild times". If a company knowingly abuses this trust, deceives its customers, i.e. its financial backers, then this is not only deeply immoral, but at the same time also a fundamental disregard for the achievements that generations of performance-hardened employees have made since the existence of a company. VW, AUDI, BMW, Mercedes have not only deceived their customers with the manipulation of exhaust values, but have also betrayed the achievements of their predecessors. This history-less action, geared exclusively to momentary success, seems typical of an attitude that measures brand success in quarters and not in generations.

3.2.2 Orientation in the Flood: Rocking Children and Checking e-Mails

Around 1900, the average American slept 10 h a night. Around 1980, the average sleep was 8 h. Today, the average person sleeps only six and a half hours. Our epoch is characterized by a comprehensive restlessness (cf. Crary 2014, p. 16). In his work on "acceleration," scholar Hartmut Rosa makes clear that a crucial imperative of the capitalist ethic is to use time as intensively as possible. This "basic experience of modernity" characterizes a comprehensive restlessness—the fear of constantly missing out on something, so that the "good life" passes us by. Although more and more helping machines accompany us in everyday life (microwaves, washing machines, etc.), we have the diffuse feeling that we have less and less time. Rosa argues that the freed-up time in the modern age does not pass "pointlessly", but is immediately used again to increase the options for action (swinging the child while checking emails on the smartphone, making phone calls, eating yoghurt, painting nails and writing WhatsApp)—multitasking. Nothing is really "off" anymore, as evidenced by the triumph of the stand-by function. This form of simultaneity requires a way of thinking that is essential for a capitalist commodity management system: the technically controlled increase in the speed of production only makes sense—and can be mapped in business terms—if the increase in the speed of distribution and, above all, consumption is achieved at the same time (cf. Rosa 2005). Marx has argued that it characterizes modernity in terms of commodity values that physical wear and tear is replaced by moral wear and tear (Marx thus anticipated the notion of product cycles). Permanent or fixed forms of production run counter to the goals of a value-added economy. Rather, production must incorporate a "planned obsolescence" of each product, which usually occurs through an expansion of options or customization possibilities. Let us look at some examples.

Examples

In 1974, the first VW Golf was produced, followed 9 years later, in 1983, by the Golf II. Eight years later, the Golf III followed. Only 6 years passed, then the Golf IV was offered. After all, it took another 6 years until the Golf V. From the Golf VI to the Golf VII it was five. The production cycle was halved, the regular revisions, so-called "facelifts", still excluded from consideration.

Today, mobile phones are rarely replaced because they no longer work, but because they are no longer the latest model—Apple thrives on this (by the way, an average German household had 400 different objects around 1900, in 2012 there are 10,000).

The German telecommunications provider 1&1 advertises 2020 with the contract offer of an annual automatic mobile phone exchange. An ideal-typical example of product devaluation commitment in "growth"-oriented markets. ◄

Former investment banker and current environmental activist Pavan Sukhdev concludes: "In classical economics, it is said that need and demand lead to innovation. The opposite is true: innovations drive demand. The reason is the advertising industry. It creates needs out of nothing, transforms the weakness and insecurity of individuals into desire—and that leads to production" (Winkelmann 2013, p. 50).

What impact does this have on our understanding of a product? The high-frequency (exchange) rhythm that applies above all to technical devices prevents us from building routines and trust with a product. While furniture or even a radio accompanied our grandparents, perhaps even our parents, through their lives and left traces as individual appliances, "grew on us", this is hardly possible with the two-year replacement of the smartphone under a framework contract or with the design- or price-oriented IKEA furniture purchase. 30-year-old IKEA furniture now even has collector value. The impact on the brand is fundamental:

> Because the product itself becomes a functional end in itself, i.e. it does not develop its own story but only functions, the brand takes on the role of permanence. I no longer buy product xy, but I buy changing products of brand xy. The shorter the life of the product, the more important the brand will become.

In order to ensure the willingness to incline towards a brand, it seems almost inevitable that a German citizen is confronted or bombarded with 3000 to 6000 advertising messages every day (depending on the study), the average supermarket offers approx. 10,000 products, 30,000 new articles in the area of so-called "fast-moving consumer goods" alone force their way onto the market every year and 35,000 brand names are registered in Europe—every year! The effects on thinking are fundamental: if everything is supposed to change constantly and if the latest thing is old in the shortest time, then the assumption that an object or an experience has a permanent value is permanently frustrated and therefore hardly formed.

Only against this background does the psychosocial "value" of the brand become clear:

- Brand creates—or more aptly: suggests—contingency.
- Brand is capable of embodying beacons of expectation-keeping, especially in a field that otherwise stands for quick-change.
- Brands are the result of services that have been successfully provided by a company over a long period of time. A collective pre-confidence is created, or to use a brand sociological term, a positive prejudice.

The presence of a positive bias distinguishes the brand from the product. Products have no preconceptions. A sleek logo, an application to the patent office or a creative advertising strategy cost a lot of money, but do not make a brand. What an incredible feat brands have achieved when complete strangers, upon mentioning a (brand) name, mention certain identical characteristics across generations and countries. It is doubtful that this could be done just as successfully with works by important artists. Audi has certainly done more for the popularity and awareness of the German language with the German phrase "Vorsprung durch Technik", which was used globally at times, than the Goethe-Institut.

3.2.3   Economics Means Fighting Prejudices

We are used to classifying prejudice as something undesirable and deeply regrettable. If there's one thing the zeitgeist doesn't allow enlightened people to do, it's to be prejudiced … at most, that's what large-scale tattooed men in undershirts and sweatpants have (watch out for prejudice!). A relic of the enlightened 1970s, in which prejudice stood in many people's minds for narrow-mindedness and intellectual and moral backwardness—although since the 1920s sociologists had always distinguished between positive and negative prejudices. Or as the sociologist Max Horkheimer found, "Without the machinery of prejudice, one could not cross the street, let alone serve a customer." (Horkheimer 1962, p. 5).

For a brand, positive prejudice is the all-important characteristic in competition. Because market economy is the competition for the strongest positive prejudice. From the perspective of brand sociology, prejudices are not undesirable phenomena, on the contrary. A brand creates a collective of people who share a Positive Prejudice regarding a particular performance. The continuous fulfilment of expectations creates a stable loyalty relationship, which is expressed on the customer side by a regular purchase. However, this also means that if a brand has collectively polarized certain characteristics, it is trapped in an irrevocable self-commitment relationship. For the testing moment in the act of purchase is never lost, even within collective structures. If a brand does not act as usual, we forgive it once, but if it occurs repeatedly, we turn away. A brand like Penny should therefore not get the idea of integrating fancy shelves made of dark precious wood into the store because it is more aesthetically pleasing and appears more valuable—that would not be "typical" Penny and would damage this economic body. A Volkswagen manager should not seriously try to offer a car called Phaeton for the price of a small terraced house under the name Volks-Wagen (now discontinued).

Whether beautiful or ugly, cheap or expensive: The redeemed trust is the real service to the clientele. Core elements of the brand are not negotiable. And when elements are up for grabs, a change in collective perception only succeeds over a long period of time. The careful repositioning of the AUDI brand from a petit bourgeois car to a premium sedan for dynamic business leaders and all those who consider themselves to be) one thinks that the occupants are completely designed and delivered with the car) over two decades makes this clear.

3.3   What Is a Brand?

So what actually is a brand? If there is already a confusion of definitions for "sustainable", "organic" or "fair", it is similar with regard to the phenomenon of brand. With the increasing atomization of social communities, the brand experiences increasing penetration and acceptance. It's amazing: many people define themselves by the car they sit in, the type of coffee that's on the table, or the logo that adorns their polo shirt. Even the greatest individualist cannot escape belonging to certain brands. Even "eco" is a brand, of course! Even a punk is subject to the stylistic commands and prohibitions of his brand of punk. Whether capitalism or socialism: in economic cycles there are no unbranded areas. People live with brands—already for centuries. Brands seem to solve or fulfill fundamental human problems and needs. Let's get a brief overview of today's understanding of brands and see how brand is explained from a sociological point of view.

3.3.1 The Trade Mark from a Legal Point of View

Trademark law is an important instrument to enable the trademark and the associated promise of performance to be assigned without irritation. However, if trademarks offer solutions for certain desires across cultures and times, this makes it clear that trademarks must be more than just a designation registered with the Trademark Office, more than "just" a legally protected trademark. In 1874, laws "On the Protection of Trade Marks" were enacted in Germany, which for the first time made it possible to protect figurative marks. However, word marks which did not consist of a company name or a name were unprotected. In 1894 the *law for the protection of trade marks* followed. This new law continued to emphasise the registration principle, but also recognised protection of figurative marks (i.e. well-known signs used in business transactions) on the basis of competition law. In addition, protection was extended to purely word marks. For the protection of trademarks or signs, a uniform register of signs was subsequently created at the newly founded Reich Patent Office for the entire territory of the German Reich. In the following decades, the laws were successively adapted to the requirements of the time.

The increasing penetration of the everyday world as well as new forms of brand presence led to a profound revision of trademark law in the 1990s. At the same time, the basic idea of legal protection remained intact: A protected name, a registered graphic sign or a sound logo represent a way of channelling the knowledge and trust placed in these symbols and the services associated with them. Thus, the legal scholar Karl-Heinz Fezer, author of the Trademark Law Commentary, had classified the trademark as a "signal code for a product for communication between actors in the marketplace" (see Harte-Bavendamm 2015, p. 79). Enacted in 1995, trademark law currently defines a trademark as follows:

> All signs, in particular words including personal names, illustrations, letters, numbers, sound signs, three-dimensional designs including the shape of a product or its packaging as well as other get-ups including colours and colour combinations, which are capable of distinguishing the goods or services of one undertaking from those of other undertakings may be protected as trade marks. (Federal Ministry of Justice and Consumer Protection n.d.)

Henning Harte-Bavendamm, lawyer and professor for copyright and competition law, states: "[...] since then, there has been an increasing awareness, also in the legal discussion, that the significance of the trademark extends far beyond its core function, namely to indicate the origin of the product or service from a particular company. Concepts such as the quality function, communication function, invest-ment function and advertising function of the trade mark have long since found their way into the case law of the Court of Justice of the European Union (CJEU)." (Harte-Bavendamm 2015, p. 80).

3.3.2   The Brand from an Economic Perspective

Economists observe the brand in the field of marketing. It is all the more astonishing that the topic of "brand management" as an explicit field of work has only become the focus of economists in the last 20–30 years. After all, company leaders, employees, inventions and production methods come and go; the only constant in strong companies is and remains the good name. Even when a company is in economic decline, the only company value that still brings in money and is therefore fervently gilded by the bankruptcy trustees is often the brand name and logo. Name rights of former brand icons such as "Grundig"or "Telefunken" were readily bought by dubious sellers and subsequently traded at a high price. Therefore, some of such former brand icons still exist as name shells, the products, however, have nothing to do with the glorious pre-performance history, but represent valuable purchasable stepping stones for market penetration in Europe, especially for producers in Asia.

Economics was comparatively late in emancipating itself from the legal concept of marking. Just over 20 years ago, Gabler's business dictionary defined brands in the following way: "Name, designation, sign, design, symbol or combination of these elements for the identification of a product (product personality) or a service of a provider and for the differentiation from competitors". (Gabler-Wirtschaftslexikon 1997, p. 2537). At the turn of the millennium, a deeper consideration of the phenomenon of brand began. Leading economists defined brand with its ability to distinguish individual products, product lines or complete assortments from similar products, to facilitate their rapid recognition in the growing multiplicity of products and brands, to make their origin visible as well as to form market or target group-specific preferences by conveying an additional benefit and to build up a unique brand image desired by the provider (cf. Esch and Wicke 2001, p. 3 ff.).

A few years earlier, the economist Heribert Meffert had already taken a turn within business management analysis and integrated aspects into an economic view that had until then—in style and thought—been novel. Meffert defines: "Brand identity is [. . .] to be understood as the sum, free of contradictions, of all characteristics of a brand, which permanently distinguishes this branded article from others and thus constitutes its brand personality." (Meffert 1998, p. 812).

However, neither jurisprudence nor economics answers the question of how this *trust,* how the "personality" in relation to a name came about—this is also not the primary task of these sciences. However, in order to understand how brands work and to satisfy the desire to strategically manage them in a way that creates value, it is fundamental to know the causal *social* cause-and-effect relationships and dynamics in order to be able to use them in brand building and brand management. Trust and personality are both categories of the social sciences. It is precisely in order to understand these connections and underlying interactions of the alliance building around a name that brand sociology provides decisive insights and parameters.

3.3.3 The Brand from a Socio-Economic Point of View

It is neither economically nor legally explainable why rational secularized people in the twenty-first century are prepared en masse to pay €159 for a pair of Hugo Boss jeans or €110 for a pair of Kuyichi jeans, although they would have to pay at most half that for a private label of a textile retailer in the same quality league (there are no jeans on the consumer markets that cost more than ten US dollars to produce). Value and cut are virtually identical to a layman's eye. The success of a range of "organic" products flies in the face of so-called homo economicus—if food were all about satiety, then a single discount brand would suffice for us all. Analytically speaking, there is no reason why humans do not simply choose the product with the best price-performance ratio when making decisions, large or small. If we were to make decisions solely rationally, it would be inexplicable why several dozen organic supermarkets exist, when really all shopping is about replenishing our life energies with food. It seems that the idea of the "consumer" does not correspond to the facts: people do not just consume instinctively, they choose as a customer of a brand. There is no such thing as the disengaged consumer; there is only the experiential observer who buys because he is accustomed to a product and its attributes associated with it—and en masse, because no brand can live on just one customer. Brand lives on the fact that many people think of its unique performance peculiarity in a certain, same-directed way.

> Brands are social phenomena—with business implications. They cannot be explained on the basis of numbers.

Basically, it is noticeable that many professionals and other observers of brands are almost exclusively concerned with the effects of a brand. However, the human being does not decide exclusively as an examining subject even in questions of business. It is not the case that we only "believe" the mere product, its performance and the price. In the simple interplay between subject and product, a connection is created that does not focus on a rational thought result, but rather integrates a testing and confirmation based on existing experiences and personal experiences.

Brands are not a special case of group formation around an idea. It doesn't matter at all whether you're dealing with a nation, a group of Karajan devotees, Starbucks fans or a popular organic farm in the neighbourhood, the same rules and dynamics of social compression always apply—even if many advertising agencies negate precisely this in order to sell trendy new customer acquisition models at a high price . . .

What Is Brand Sociology?
Brand sociology is a science that works out lawful patterns of customer formation around a brand on the basis of socio-empirical observations. These results make it possible to make predictions with regard to the future behaviour of groups: If brand X acts in a certain way in the market, then the following effects in the clientele are very likely to occur. This scientific claim is made by a brand sociological approach because group behaviour is included in the analysis process as an empirical variable.

When many people want something in common, e.g. by putting a certain product in their shopping cart, it is a process that can be explained sociologically. The brand as a social phenomenon can be explained because it is illuminated why some people "swear by a brand", indeed remain loyal to their brand even when a variety of counter-arguments are mentioned, and show displeasure, unwillingness or rejection towards other brands—without real knowledge.

The theory behind this understanding of group formation around ideas was laid down by the founding father of German sociology, Ferdinand Tönnies, as early as 1887 in his book Gemeinschaft und Gesellschaft. What exactly does Tönnies understand by the common will? First of all, he assumes that an alliance only comes into being when people act conducively and helpfully with one another. Only when people—as Tönnies puts it—relate to each other in an *affirmative way* does the brand sociologist speak of an alliance. Social thus does not already take place when two people meet by chance, but only when I, as an individual, decide to cooperate with others. Social is therefore always intentional. In this context, it is initially irrelevant whether I decide to marry or to buy a piece of chewing gum at a kiosk. In both situations I purposefully enter into a relationship with a counterpart—of course to a different degree of density (if things go well). However, in the scientific understanding, social is not a category of "being good to each other". Initially, social simply means that one is in a relationship with one another. The goals of this cooperation can be terrible or destructive to other people: The members of a gang of criminals who decide to rob a jeweller's shop together are—considered in themselves—certainly in a beneficial social relationship with each other, but act in a highly destructive way in relation to others.

Alliances permeate life permanently: friends, family, work colleagues, the trip to the holidays. Each time, we have chosen to cooperate with other people at some point. Importantly, people form alliances not only with other people, but often with things. The fact that I choose a particular beer puts me in a beneficial relationship with the brewery I've chosen, the way it's produced, and the people who work there. This relationship is not abstract, but very concrete, in that the company receives money from me.

This social will is multifaceted. It occurs in two ideal types: The *essential will* and the *arbitrary will.* These two forms differ in their recourse to rational drives on the one hand and more subconscious-emotional drives on the other.

The Arbitrary Will
The arbitrary will is characterized by abstract, logical, purely objective considerations. An illustrative model of arbitrary will is the concept of "homo oeconomicus" used in business administration. This ideal market participant acts purely rationally, independently and does not rest until he has found optimal solutions for his plans. All decisions are based on a stringent analysis of effort and benefit with the aim of realizing personal needs with the lowest possible investment: I decide in a certain way because I expect a certain outcome with a high probability in the future.

In the context of the brand, products purchased willingly are usually "reasonable" products. People buy something because it has proven to be particularly "solution-oriented" (for example, good test results), because it is particularly "inexpensive" or because they are looking for an alternative.

The Essential Will
Man never decides exclusively rationally. While the arbitrary will is in principle based on a conscious thought process, the essential will is the organically grown result of cultural and biographical life contexts in which we grow up. In contrast to an intellectual judgment, the essential will to be can hardly be explained causally: it is emotionally shaped. Everything that a person wants out of himself, following his nature, falls under this category. Essential will arises from accumulated experiences over time. Thus, the relationship in families or the relationship with friends is characterized by a high degree of volitional manners. Thinking with a will to be is instinctive and usually even eludes our own conscious basis for decision-making.

Products we buy for years and even decades don't follow rational scrutiny—at some point, a certain chocolate spread is part of our breakfast. The Siemens company postulated the slogan: "We belong to the family." Miele skillfully makes the new washing machine a member of the family in their billboard advertising. Some brands have become part of our identity and are bought even though there may be rational reasons (e.g. price) against it.

It is decisive that both forms of will do not occur absolutely in the reality of life. For brand sociology, they are scientific categories that always occur mixed together in reality—in varying proportions. No favourite product can win only by being "loved". It must also perform. And a willing act of purchase will not succeed if we do not develop a minimum of emotional affection for the product.

Will Creates Alliances
The forms of will described form the basis for two types of social bonds that people enter into with other people or with things. Tönnies differentiates between community and society. Communities are characterized by many individuals who meet each other willingly. Society is characterized by arbitrary will, i.e. the purposefulness of encounters. Thus, life in community is shaped by shared beliefs, unwritten rules, and familiarity. Much is because it already was. Society is characterized by a purposefulness that flexibly adapts to changing circumstances and freely chooses its members according to their goals. Much is because it is supposed to be.

While community is symbolically based on the handshake, the binding medium in society is the contract. The differentiation of community and society is more than a historical characterization, for it denotes the way in which we encounter alliances or groups. Cooperatives are—ideally speaking—community-oriented alliances, whereas a corporation focuses on short-term purpose. Whether a company is more community- or society-oriented, whether FC Bayern München, for example, is still a genuine community or more of a society, has fundamental effects on how we encounter a range of goods. Because goods or services also form groups at the moment they appear. The question for management around a performance idea is: are we more community driven or more society driven? What is clear is:

> The more common structures prevail, the stronger the binding power of the brand.

Communities

We are inevitably born into community—whether we are born in Berlin, Boston or Buenos Aires will shape our mother tongue, our cultural practices and our view of the world. Communities are characterized by a strong connection through similar socialization and collective memories. The community is a community of destiny that has emerged from the past and whose traces guide our decisions. How something should be determines how we live together, although the contents are usually not documented anywhere in writing. That is why the community makes to a large extent unfree. It is not we who speak "German", but "the German" that speaks from us. Only because we submit to the grammar and phonetics of a language are we able to communicate. The linguist Guy Deutscher holds:

> Language has two lives: In its public role, it is a system of conventions agreed upon by a speech community for the purpose of effective communication. But language also has another, private existence as a system of knowledge that each individual speaker has internalized in his or her mind. If language is to serve as an effective means of communication, then the private system of knowledge in the minds of speakers must correspond pretty closely to the public system of linguistic conventions. (Deutscher 2012, p. 266)

Communities are extremely stable due to their organic connectedness—a family community, for example, is more stable than the relationship to a company in which one works. The reason for this is that, ideally, the familiarity of togetherness in a community creates trust. Membership of a family cannot be terminated, even if one breaks away from it. When the going gets tough, you stand together again. Accordingly, the founder of brand sociology Alexander Deichsel writes, "Community is sometimes agonizing, annoyingly pleasurable, but uniquely securing." (Deichsel 2006, p. 57). Within it operates a social force known as custom. Into it man inevitably grows. For: what is natural for us is always what we are familiar with.

Companies

The members of societies want to realize certain objectives together. Once this is done, the association dissolves. The individual has the possibility to freely determine his goals and acts autonomously. In societies, decisions are basically made according to rational motives, generally valid rules are formulated. All decisions are based on one's own individual decisions and agreements. The contract is the decisive tool of social processes. Society thus acts as an antithesis to the community, which reduces the freedom of the individual and integrates him into its social structure by means of collectively enforced norms.

Brand and Product = Community and Society
What both a social and a communal association have in common is that a social body emerges from the conducive interaction of its members. The moment people are attracted to an idea and group around it, the brand sociologist speaks of a social or system body. It is irrelevant whether people find a particular brand of lemonade fascinating, a sports club or a restaurant. The way a drink is created or how it tastes, the fan culture or the friendliness of the landlord are typical motivations to support this performance body with money, time and interest—for personal well-being.

In the understanding of brand sociology, the market is nothing other than the result of an infinite number of service offers. Because many people in different positions work to ensure that there is a football club in St. Pauli, an FC St. Pauli is created—supported by investors, by players or coaches and finally by the spectators who are prepared to support the club by buying a ticket and chanting loudly. The result of this will of different people at different points of contact creates a concretely perceptible performance system. It is special in itself. It structures the environment in a certain, in the best case recognizable, typical way. FC St. Pauli is not the FC Barcelona. There are good reasons for everyone to be a fan of one sports club and not the other. The fact that he eventually became one is because the range of services was specific and distinctive.

Performance systems are horizons of possible action—never arbitrary, but always defined. Every brand is grouped around a clear centre of will. It radiates a clear impulse with its interpretation of how the world should be at a certain point. The people who follow this impulse no longer act as unattached individuals, but they act *in* something that stylistically dictates their actions. This distinction is essential in terms of brand sociology: many managers are accustomed to describing a brand in terms of its sales figures, its customer groups, its competition, its "reason-why" through very detailed market research and market observation. Very often there is a belief that the information obtained captures the essence of the object. The problem, however, is that the data at hand are nothing more than descriptions *about* something. They do not describe the object itself. Things are described in detail, but not explained. If one were to put together the information and data received, the result would not be the object itself. The decisive task is to penetrate to the actual core of the performance body. This means describing it from the inside out and first and foremost grasping its normative characteristics. This distinction is important because it describes the dividing line between work on the surface of a brand, i.e. on its effects or the analysis of its performance causes, and its substance. Only the clear separation of a brand's effects and its causes makes the individual performance body recognizable and thus manageable. Therefore:

The decisive question that arises in the case of the analysis of brands is always which are the respective underlying operating principles.

> **How Does a Brand Interpret Its Performance Field Over Time?**
> Celebrity lounge or standing room in the football stadium—is this all about football? Personal greeting at the table or plastic card at the restaurant entrance—it's all about food? Welcome cards in the room or computer check-in at the hotel—it's only about an overnight stay? Each of these specific patterns defines a performance system. Very often we talk about people's *perceptions in* relation to a brand, but it is crucial to reverse the view and ask much more what the *perception is that* is being targeted. After all, it is the reason why people choose a certain brand or not. Acknowledgement of oneself is the condition for recognition. Because everything recognizable is always stable. Brands are thus social thought constructs, polarized ideas of individuals that are supposed to occur in such a way and only in such a way. The brand Teekampagne, for example, is limited to two products: green and black Darjeeling tea. A clear image is created in public, irritating complexity is avoided.

Brand Is Shape

A body of performance is recognizable only when it differs from its environment, when it follows certain recurring rules and commandments, that is, when it has assumed a specific shape. Only a specific gestalt is able to interest and attract certain people, for exactly the same reasons it repels other people.

For a brand, design ideas are often found at the foundation of the company: a typical origin, the history and origins of the founders, specific raw materials and certain expertise in production and processing, questions of distribution—all these are characteristics that make a design system perceptible and recognizable. Brand is therefore not created in a product development, in a laboratory, in an advertising agency, but it is always the result of a social interaction between idea and people.

The term Gestalt makes a crucial connection clear: Gestalt means the ability of humans to immediately and unconsciously form an overall perception from the perception of various details that occur in isolation from one another: We see a person, his clothes, his gait, his facial expression, and cannot help finding this person friendly or unsympathetic. This anthropological talent of humans to compose an overarching perception from information is what makes survival in a complex world possible in the first place. Because the quick classification of impressions allows us to recognize opportunities as well as dangers (Errichiello 2021).

Brands Are Cultural Bodies

What does this mean for a brand sociological perspective? By classifying certain perceptions in a variety of ways, we orient ourselves in a profoundly confusing world. As cultural beings, our thinking is never free, but always bound up in collective experiential values that provide orientation. From the way a person speaks or dresses, we draw certain conclusions, use "mental pigeonholes"—even if we, as enlightened people, would like to resist them. Humans permanently act in these categorization structures.

Psychologists make it clear time and again that a basic constant of human existence is that we want to be perceived as persons. This is why the business class stewardess addresses each of her passengers by name. Because we live only once and the prospect of the afterlife is considered rather unlikely in times of secularization, it is all the more important to appear outwardly as individuals in the limited decades of our existence. Very few people succeed in making their own path in life recognizable through artistic masterpieces or particularly outstanding economic successes. In their study "The Narcissism Epidemic" (2010), social scientists Jean M. Twenge and W. Keith Campbell conducted numerous surveys on Americans' self-esteem. Among other things, they found that when asked the simple question "Are you an important person?" more than 80 percent of all 14- to 16-year-olds answered "yes," up from 12 percent in 1950. The fact that nowadays "voting" is commonplace in everything from talent shows to doctors' treatment to university professors, supposedly to improve "quality", has another reason: the individual and his or her opinion are to be taken into account. Whether the individual even has a basis for his opinion on the subject is not asked.

The branded article steps into this socio-psychological breach, because by buying a certain product with a good name I become recognisable as an individual. The branded article thus resolves the contradiction between individuality and mass. The brand gives the individual the material to become himself. Or: The product is the basis for every individuation. It is no coincidence that one of the most successful brand series in history starts with "i": iPhone, iMac, iPod, etc. One can personally regret this and point out the wickedness of the consumer industry, but the notion that we act as autonomous beings is more lofty ideal than reality. The French philosopher Alain Finkielkraut writes: "As far back as one goes in history, it is not society that is born of man, but the latter is born into a particular society. From the very beginning, he is forced to incorporate his actions, just as he situates his speech and thought in a language that has developed without him and that is beyond his power. From the very beginning: For whether it is a question of his nation or of his language, man enters into a game in which it is not for him to make the rules, but for him to learn and keep them." (Cf. Errichiello and Zschiesche 2011, p. 16).

Precisely because almost all areas of our lives are filled by and with branded goods, we cannot exclude their predisposing effect on perception and behaviour. The capitalist-dynamized world of goods is all-encompassing—non-consumption is not possible (except for some highly individual niche life designs). Life is consumption—consumption is life . . . as frustrating as it may be for the individual.

Brands make use of this will to compose and the culture-bound nature of people. Alexander Deichsel clearly formulates: "We gather things around us because they have meaning for us. They tell us a lot about ourselves and others. In our attachments, things play an essential role." (Deichsel 2006, p. 47). Brand characterizes that it has a clearly defined content for me and others, that is, it is able to tell people a clear, recognizable story.

It is through these stories that we individualize ourselves as customers. By shopping at Alnatura, wearing a T-shirt from Patagonia and driving a Toyota Prius, our self is created. We use charged symbols to construct our selves. The social psychologist Erich Fromm wrote, that we "think [learn] by observing others and being taught by them. We develop our emotional, intellectual, and artistic capacities by coming into contact with the accumulated knowledge and artistic achievements created by society." (Errichiello and Zschiesche 2011, p. 14).

Individual Through Mass
In essence, mass-produced goods substitute for the desire for individuality, because brands offer us the material for individualization. The relationship between mass and individual is seen as describing two extremes. The mass would depersonalize the individual, but as "Germans", "Berliners" or "Greens" we are constantly members of masses. In the brand, this aspect becomes particularly obvious. By choosing products and services with a message character whose contents are as widely known as possible ("I wear Knowledge Cotton Apparel and not Superdry" or "Only fair trade"), we become perceivable as individual beings. From the thousands of consumption choices, the person emerges. But beware: the individual choice of content is free, because no one can force us to like the color "blue" or to have any particular taste. Immanuel Kant justified this in the introduction to the "Critique of the Power of Judgement" as follows: "An aesthetic judgement in general can therefore be declared to be that judgement whose predicate can never be cognition (concept of an object) (although it may contain the subjective conditions for cognition at all). In such a judgment, the determinant is sensation. Now there is only one so-called sensation that can never become a concept of an object, and this is the feeling of pleasure and displeasure." (Kant 1990, p. 30 f.)

The result is that the mass article does not unify, but individualizes. Brands are the right to inequality. It is this logic that explains the inexorable rise of the brand over the past 100 years.

As people of the twenty-first century, we are part of a confusing number of masses every day: We get up in the morning and are a customer of the waterworks while showering, a father while admonishing the children to "finally get dressed", a husband while kissing his wife goodbye, then a car driver and a listener of BBC … Constantly, in the westernized world, we are connected to social masses or circles, in which we constantly enter and exit, but to which we submit in their style and expression.

Prejudices: The Decisive Competitive Weapon
Building trust in an offer requires positive experiences that are as free of irritation as possible. If a brand maintains its appearance in typical quality, language and appearance in certain stores for decades, a clear image is polarized in people's minds. The Positive Prejudice that is created in the best case is constitutive for the

existence of a brand. A brand exists when there is agreement among the public relevant to the product about the characteristics of the offering.

A prejudice in the scientific sense is a judgment that people make on the basis of information and generally project onto an object. A forefather of prejudice research, the American Gordon W. Allport, defined it in 1954: "Perhaps the shortest of all definitions of prejudice is: Thinking ill of others without sufficient justification. This terse formulation contains the two essential elements of all relevant definitions: the reference to the unfoundedness of the judgment and to the feeling tone. It is, however, too brief for complete clarity. First of all, this formulation refers to negative prejudice. But some also have positive prejudices about others." (Allport 1971, p. 20).

The following applies to brand management: Market economy is the battle for the strongest prejudice. Prejudices fulfil—from a scientific point of view—a social function. Because they provide orientation and the possibility to make quick decisions in an increasingly unmanageable environment. Humans are not capable of living and socializing without prejudices. In every area of our lives we act on the basis of positive and negative prejudices.

Prejudices are the result of social will within a community. These socially "charged" and extremely stable contents work across a group and are able to reduce the individual's ability to criticize. Thus, we blindly reach for the shelf at our favorite brands and trust that everything will be the same as always. An unconscious immaturity occurs, which conditions the actual brand value: the more unconsciously the decision for a brand is made, the stronger the brand power is. The French economist Jean-Noel Kapferer states: "Brand is a reference, but also a signal, which is recognized due to a unique composition of visual elements (packaging shape, color scheme, distribution of graphic masses, logo, name). It is also a contract: over time, a trademark becomes a promise of high quality and a specific performance. This gives the brand, especially the big brand, very high appeal." (Kapferer 1997, p. 1).

Positive preconceptions are the basis of every successful branding and transform the initially unknown product into a brand with message character through experience. Once this brand state has been achieved, the customer's commitment to the purchase is minimized because there is no need to compare and weigh. The following applies here:

Positive Prejudice is never created by advertising, but by performance. The mere awareness of a brand name does not say anything about whether the relevant people also associate a positive prejudice of the same direction with this name. Only when this has been achieved do we speak of brands.

To claim an achievement or to make a name known by means of massive advertising efforts is an interesting thing—to convince other people permanently of an achievement is something completely different.

Success Principle Self-Similarity: Strong Brands Act Self-Similarly
A brand based solely on advertising will not last long. Factually perceptible proof of performance is crucial to win customers for a brand. Every specialist salesman in

direct customer contact knows that he can never convince his customers with abstract and unspecific information. If his counterpart is interested in buying a car, then pretty image brochures and fancy TV commercials are of little use. Facts count when it comes to persuasion: Price, consumption, technical features, even the sound of the doors closing and the glove compartment. Even an employee for a green bank is not won over at the beginning by "a good feeling" alone and brochures with lots of trees on glossy paper. What matters is how the bank handles money, what projects it finances and how it provides information about them. Often it is not even this, but the personality and person of the advisor who leaves a trusting impression in direct contact (which is difficult to prescribe and cannot be "commanded" even by 100 training sessions).

Decisive for whether a brand behaves energetically is the question whether it acts "typically". The normative power to permanently follow its own design rules is what brand sociology calls self-similarity. Thus, for an Erdkorn supermarket it does not matter whether it is located in Berlin or Hamburg: In the best case, we enter the store and it is immediately clear from the design, the appearance of the employees and from the assortment: this is an Erdkorn supermarket (slogan: "Organic from my region."). The individual design elements of the "Erdkorn" brand appear coherent with each other and "fit together"—far beyond the design elements.

The principle of self-similarity comes from fractal geometry. This means that certain systems only change in terms of their size, but not in terms of their structure. The bodies known as fractals can be perceived everywhere in nature: for example, thousands of leaves can be found on every oak tree. None of these leaves is identical to another in shape, but all are nevertheless recognizable in themselves as leaves of an oak tree. For social systems, this means that each part of the whole always carries the idea of the whole system. The Nobel Prize winner for physics, Gerd Binnig, makes it clear that self-similarity is a basic principle for evolutionary processes: "We found Darwinian processes such as reproduction, mutation and selection everywhere. We found everywhere the building block character and directed action, which we defined as a self-limitation of a system to a field of possibility." (Cf. Deichsel 2006, p. 162).

Self-similarity is the *natural* counter-program to an identical reproduction of systems. The idea of managing a brand in terms of a corporate identity is problematic because this means not making adjustments and changes. No two leaves of an oak tree are the same because nutrient supply, sunlight and wind conditions on a tree differ and require different adaptation. Maybe different products sell better in Munich than in an organic market in Hamburg? Of course, a company has to take this into account and adapt, but only to the extent that both ranges continue to be "typical" for the brand.

Strong brands never act identically, but always self-similarly, because a brand must adapt to changing technical or social developments, but always remain true to itself. In doing so, the individual elements, such as employees, raw materials or processing, can constantly exchange and, in the best case, optimize themselves. It is important to remember that all strong brands replace their customers several times in the course of their life cycle—naturally. At Persil, we have not only known what we have since 1907, our advertising once said: "Every generation has its Persil". One of the oldest brands in the world, the Catholic Church, has already replaced its customers 60 to 70 times since it was founded more than 2000 years ago, and a brand icon like Coca-Cola has replaced its customers four to five times. Both brand systems have not changed their essence since then, although the original constituent elements have long since crumbled to dust … Strong brands have never suspended or abandoned their core idea, their original idea—otherwise they would never have developed brand character, i.e. prejudices. In this logic, the American marketing pioneer David A. Aaker formulates: "[…] brands do not exist in a time capsule." (Aaker 1997, p. 110).

Self-similarity encompasses all areas of the brand that can be experienced by an observer and buyer. It applies:

Any successful brand system must be clearly identifiable everywhere, because it exists only as a unique system.

The advantages of self-similar brand management are clear: brand systems remain viable because they remain true to themselves even when the zeitgeist changes and do not make themselves unrecognizable by adapting. In addition, a self-similar brand can build on the trust and knowledge of its customers on the basis of its fixed character and therefore requires much less energy to explain the product and its characteristics. The brand sociologist Klaus Brandmeyer explains: "If, and only if, a brand presents itself to its customers in the same form over a longer period of time, and not in a new, surprising, different form every day, people get used to its shapes, colors, sounds, scents, gestures and messages. Only in this way can a relationship build and familiarity develop." (Brandmeyer 1999, p. 397).

Customer trust requires appreciation—and only those things have value for me that accompany me consistently and offer me performance security. Appreciation is the basis for the willingness to pay "more". Because the brand is able to preserve and communicate its distinctive features, the customer has an increased inclination to value the product/service offered more highly than the money he invests. The purchase is a gain despite the factual loss of money. This psychological starting point makes it clear why brand must always make it concretely clear why it is worth the money. In doing so, it is not crucial to offer as much as possible, because that makes a brand unspecific, but on the contrary to concentrate on the essential factors of one's own success. A consistent consideration of this basic rule of brand sociology has dramatic effects on the understanding of brand activities that is widespread today: All strategies must no longer be oriented towards supposed trends, personal opinions and preferences, short-term windfall effects, ominous "market requirements" or so-called "benchmarks", but solely towards the question of whether the self-similar genetics of the brand are realized or strengthened.

Market Research as Brand Killer

Market research is a particular source of danger for the brand: information about "the market" is constantly pelting down on those responsible. If the market moves into the focus of attention, perhaps even dictates the brand strategy, the specificity inevitably dissolves. Because the market does not orient itself to the special features of a brand. If we ask people in a pedestrian zone what they think of the brand Weleda, connoisseurs will talk about anthroposophy, some will say that the brand offers high-quality products which are, however, too expensive, and so on. But can all these statements be serious parameters for a future brand strategy? Most likely, for example, the high price is a decisive component of the brand's success, because it makes the quality claim factual and the clientele has perceived this brand component for decades: "With the price, respect increases", say the respectable merchant as well as the respectable brand sociologist: The Weleda brand must therefore rigorously pay attention to enforcing the price for its products and not introduce a cheap line.

> Any brand that adapts to the "market" without preserving its genetic code will dissolve.

Adapting to the market means doing what everyone else is doing. Because today, in the major industries, you can safely assume that all potent competitors are observing and "ploughing" the same market via market research. In every marketing department there are ambitious employees willing to work for it, who want to achieve the best result for their company because it gives them pleasure—or just because they want to afford a gas grill for their success bonus. When presented with the same results across an entire industry, very similar results and actions are usually derived . . . with the result that everyone becomes aligned and products become interchangeable. That which brands are supposed to be, namely the special, the special impulse that causes the purchase decision, is lost. And if there are no more performance-specific differences, the price is the only remaining distinguishing feature. This is exactly the bankruptcy of brand management.

> Those who do not take into account their own history and thus their identity will make themselves the same. The result: interchangeability—the death sentence for every brand.

It is necessary to react to changing environmental and general conditions in a "typical" way. The question of what exactly this brand typicality comprises makes brand management a sensitive management theory that must analytically grasp the typical i.e. specific structure of a brand. Self-similar brand management is never stagnation, on the contrary, it requires a perpetual interpretation of external change processes from a fixed point of view. If a company has a loyal customer base, the brand's primary obligation is to meet the community's expectations and offer a consistent body of services. In this regard, however, the reverse is also true:

> Brands must clearly define what they are not. Employees and customers must always know what the brand does not offer. Only this clear demarcation, the no, allows profile to emerge.

What is the consequence? New benefits, products or services can only profit from built-up brand power if they fit the existing Positive Prejudice, the genetic code of the brand. They even have to: Not only that a brand that does not use its existing Positive Prejudice acts highly inefficiently: In addition, inappropriate performances also destroy the already existing Prejudice in the long run, so that in the end no one knows anymore what the brand actually stands for.

3.4   Brand Is This

Brands often deliberately evade examination on the basis of economic key figures. Nevertheless, the brand is considered a genuinely economic object that could be controlled with the instruments and methods of economists. As science journalist Mitchell Waldrop points out, "Just as physicists can predict how a particle will react to given forces, economists could predict how the businessman will react to a given economic situation: He simply optimizes his 'utility function'. Neoclassical economics also describes a society where the economy always remains in perfect equilibrium, where supply always exactly matches demand, where the stock market is never shaken by price rises or crashes, where no firm ever grows so large that it dominates the market, and where the magic power of a free market turns everything around for the best." (Waldrop 1993, p. 27). By nurturing this belief, it proves to be a myth. The German philosopher Ralf Konersmann has written the following about the essence of myth: "Myth speaks of things which, in any case, we did not make and for which we therefore do not have to bear any responsibility, but which we can just as little access and change. The world of myth is the world of 'That's the way it is and that's the way it stays', and far from doubts and criticism, the rule of reception of myth provides for letting things be said once and for all." (Konersmann 2015, p. 74).

It has become clear that this absolute understanding of brands is common, but extremely problematic. Brands are not simple, linear systems—ever. This is clear from the observation alone that it is very difficult to predict exactly which brand will prove particularly successful in the market. No one could predict the rise of Apple: too expensive, technically incompatible with other systems, too selective in distribution. Taking into account pure company and market data, brand success is not comprehensible or even illogical.

The difficulty of brand management lies in the fact that at the moment when people interact with people or people interact with products, a living system is created and the dynamics within this social body (e.g. a brand) cannot be fully mapped. In contrast to inanimate systems (e.g. a machine or software, so-called trivial systems), whose internal interaction is clearly regulated and which thus produce defined results (but cannot adapt to changing market conditions), living systems consist of an innumerable number of elements that are difficult to predict. If people are involved in a project, a single emotional misunderstanding can immediately lead to friction and energy losses, which in turn have a direct impact on the system. Accordingly, living systems have a much higher degree of complexity than trivial systems and must be more comprehensively controlled and managed. As one of the first scientists, the British economist Brian Arthur dealt with the complexity of economic life, which was hardly compatible with classical economics and business administration doctrine (Waldrop 1993). In almost all variants, conventional economic doctrines assume that economic systems follow deterministic, i.e. unambiguously predictable, dynamics. In this context, economic systems are characterized by the idea that the "best idea" would generally prevail. But how can it be explained that IBM still claimed in 1950 that there would never be more than 18 computers in the USA?

Waldrop explains another example catchily: "Towards the end of the 19th century [...] petrol had little prospect of becoming the fuel of the future in the eyes of contemporaries. Its main rival, steam power, was sophisticated, familiar and safe. Gasoline, on the other hand, was expensive, noisy, could explode dangerously, had to have the right octane rating, and needed an entirely different engine with complicated new parts. Gasoline engines were also much less efficient. If things had been different, and steam engines could have benefited as much from ninety years of development as gasoline engines, we could live today with much less air pollution, and our economy would be much less dependent on oil. But gasoline prevailed—in large part, at least in the United States, because of a series of historical coincidences. [...] then foot-and-mouth disease broke out in North America in 1914, which led to the removal of horse troughs—and that was the only place where steam cars could replenish water." (Waldrop 1993, p. 52).

Complex systems are thus characterized by constant renewal. In short: Evolution permanently strives for improvements, not for perfection. Arthur was able to demonstrate that economic history has not always promoted the "best" solution: "If it depends on small random events which of several possible outcomes actually 'clicks into place', the outcome thus selected may not be the best. The greatest possible individual freedom—and the free market—do not then necessarily lead to the best of all possible worlds." (Waldrop 1993, p. 52). The notion of completely rational decisions (keyword: homo economicus) follows classical physics, however elementary particles have no past and no experience. Science journalist Waldrop therefore states: "The crucial problem, of course, is that people's actions are neither fully rational nor fully predictable [...]. And even if one assumed that people act completely rationally, the belief in perfect predictions could lead into dangerous, theoretical traps. In nonlinear systems—and the economy is surely nonlinear—the slightest uncertainty in the knowledge of the initial conditions can have tremendous effects, as chaos theory shows." (Waldrop 1993, p. 52). In an effort to make business administration a "hard" science, this discipline constantly strove to derive "regularities" that did not allow for any variations. Against this background, mathematical-physical "proofs" formed the basic understanding ... and this science increasingly distanced itself from reality in this economically decisive area—mindful of the fact that a brand analysis is primarily about taking into account the social area of experience and knowledge consolidation of collective systems and integrating it into the brand management processes in order to succeed in business management terms.

Brand is not a value in itself. Brand is the decisive means to increase the value creation power permanently and significantly. It must never be a creative playground. In order to build brand power, a company must cultivate its service-specific characteristics. A brand is only recognizable in a certain area and stands for something. It is only this premise that prevents the exclusively "rational" consideration of a product in favor of an emotional (price-insensitive) affection. If one looks at surveys, it becomes clear that the willingness to pay more for a "special quality" is still pronounced in the twenty-first century. The more the price war and an aggressive sales style become rampant, the more the clear "quality approach" is appreciated. In most cases, it is also the only one that still allows real profits and secures a company in the long term.

Brand means to offer an immaterial added value independent of the actual product benefit, which, however, is rooted in the specificity of the company or the product. An "added value" which is only the result of an ambitious advertising strategy, i.e. which is not deposited in a service-specific way, may attract attention for a short time, but in the long run such an approach leads to collapse. When observing brands, it is interesting to note that it is precisely those products/services that have a higher affinity to the brand which have a high degree of exchange in their service structure (for example drinks, instant soups, fruit). In order to achieve profits at all and to escape the ruinous comparative parameter "price", the brand must necessarily be used here. People like to talk about changed customer behaviour, the new extremely price-driven sales channels (Internet) or a lack of customer loyalty. Certainly, the markets have changed dramatically in the past 15 years—the critical question to be asked at this point is whether and to what extent one's own brand has remained true to itself in the past 15 years. The adage that you are only true to those who remain true to themselves must be the starting point when asking how you have responded to changing market conditions. In short, how has the brand itself dealt with change in recent years? Was the "brand" enforced in a self-similar way or did it often—too often—adapt to supposed market laws and become alien-like and thus interchangeable?

Brand is not a "black box", not a diffuse emotional world, but a state of affairs that can be described in detail with the instruments of brand sociology. When people support each other under the umbrella of a brand, a living system with its own rules and prohibitions is created. As a system, the brand is subject to the identical structural rules as any other power body (family, country, people)—certain signals lead to its consolidation or weakening. Strong brands benefit from high self-similarity and self-referentiality. Changes in the environment are interpreted by strong brands in such a way that they continue to fit the performance structure of the system.

3.4.1 Abstract Means Nothing

Brand sociological brand development is not oriented towards business trends or best practices, but focuses on each brand individually. There are no generally valid rules of action for brands, but rather certain effective laws of brand strengthening, which, however, follow the individual biography of the company in their interpretation. Against this background of brand sociology, not only is the primary orientation towards market research studies highly value-destroying, it is equally dangerous if a brand does not orient itself towards the causes of success, i.e. its special features, but exclusively towards its effects.

Far too often, self-descriptions, corporate philosophies or brand visions and briefing documents include the following attributes that are supposed to be the basis for a brand strategy.

Brand x defined:

- Quality
- Tradition
- Innovation
- Service orientation
- Sustainability
- Competence

An Internet search of suppliers in certain industries reveals more than 90% of these characterizations on the website "About us"—a fiasco. It is a truism that a company should produce properly, i.e. in a qualitatively appealing manner. Service orientation also says nothing—otherwise, how and on what should a company orient itself? One thing is clear: if you didn't know who was presenting themselves here with these self-descriptions, these characteristics could also stand for any competing company. Basically, companies say nothing at this point. They are the opposite of a brand because they hide behind an abstract statement of intent. Terminology is used that is in no way capable of representing the specifics of the company. As if this were not annoying enough—after all, one's own web presence is a place where the company can present itself for virtually nothing—companies use these self-descriptions in their market research categories or their briefing documents to make strategic decisions: The content of the next commercial, future ads or posters, or costly events are created based on a brand definition that defines purely nothing. What exactly is to be understood by quality may be interpreted individually by each service provider; the question of when service orientation actually exists has a wide range. In addition, the definition of quality for a chicken snack bar certainly takes other aspects into account than for a gourmet restaurant.

What does this mean? So-called brand definitions that refer solely to abstract image values weaken or stop brand development. They allow interpretations and thus deviations. The goal remains that the thinking of the public pays in again and again on anchored imaginary worlds.

Example

A brand like Weleda would certainly be graspable under the definition *"Weleda = Nature's Protector ... "*, but can such a definition actually provide guidelines for action? Aren't the highest degrees of interpretation still possible in the day-to-day business of this definition? Does "close to nature protector" mean that the brand should change its logo or that every product of the brand has to fulfil certain ecological criteria or that it only has to make clear the will to act ecologically?

EON would probably also claim to be close to nature—after all, the company also uses solar energy . . .

In terms of brand sociology, the actual brand work begins with the definition given in the example:

- What exactly does "protect" mean for Weleda?
- Through which—for the customer noticeable—performance aspects does it protect its customers?
- What does close to nature mean for the brand?

In dealing with these questions, concrete performance characteristics will emerge that make Weleda—quite unmistakably—Weleda.

At this point, an elaborate detail work begins, which extends to the individual ingredients and their mixture. This is work that most companies do not want to do or that is not considered "relevant". ◄

3.4.2 Only Limit Creates Power

When it comes to fundamentally strengthening a brand in the public eye, the key is to make a statement—to stand for something. The only way a brand can maintain its stability and appeal is by distinguishing itself from other performance systems. It is not a question of only "elite" brands being able to distinguish themselves; boundaries are a vital component of every brand system. Even an organic grocer at the weekly market distinguishes himself from the "conventional" vegetable sellers by hanging a sign "Exclusively organically controlled vegetables" on the stand. It is not the difference between upstairs and downstairs, but also between Puma /Nike, Lidl /Aldi, McDonald's or Burger King—in other words, a horizontal demarcation. What people buy in many cases in terms of distinction is not the different functionality, but the style, the way of interpreting the world. Only the particular can satisfy people's need for distinction. Ensuring this specialness is the primary task of the company.

> Every performance can become a brand. Boundary is the basis for the perception of a performance.

Or: If you want to be everything, you are nothing. The following continues to apply: "If a service under a name becomes arbitrary, if the stylistic boundary fence becomes holey, brand power automatically escapes because the company becomes interchangeable. Differentiation is and remains one of the strongest means of distinguishing oneself from others. Only compression creates attraction." (Errichiello and Zschiesche 2013, p. 73).

Brand sociology is a fact-oriented science. It transfers the comprehensibility and regularity of certain results to a factual situation which today is mainly derived from individual psychology. When it comes to questions of brand management or brand communication, decision factors are introduced with "I believe . . .", "I think . . .", "I feel . . .". These statements automatically make it clear that the argumentation here is no longer scientific-analytical, but solely based on a personal or aesthetic feeling. The following is also interesting: In an age in which managerial high performers in particular like to pretend that every one of their decisions was made purely analytically on the basis of facts, the brand is given astonishingly creative leeway—usually with the result of its massive weakening.

Brands are subject to their own performance biography, their own design rules, their own social genetics. Whether a product, a poster or a slogan is suitable for a brand can only be answered in a well-founded manner if it has been analytically worked out beforehand which individual performance components constitute the brand. Only on the basis of this individual "coordinate system" is it possible to assess whether the communication measure at hand is suitable for strengthening the positive prejudice with regard to a name or whether—on the contrary—it runs counter to the previous performance structures and thus discharges the brand power.

3.4.3 Compressing Power

Brand management is never a "creative wish concert", but exactly the opposite: serious brand management requires to a large extent the withdrawal of one's own, personal feelings and the interpretation of what already exists—in terms of brand sociology, creativity does not mean the breaking of boundaries, but the filling of clear boundaries. Long-term brand management also requires humility towards those who conceived and realised a performance idea in a specific way.

Does this approach imply that communicative brand work must be a list of hard facts and not allow any creativity? That such communication must necessarily spread the charm of a medicine package insert? Certainly there are brands that even have to consciously forego a pronounced creative excellence for the sake of strengthening the brand.

In the majority of cases, however, a company wants to advertise in a fitting and appealing way. It is true: performance-related advertising can certainly be creative, funny and rousing, as long as it focuses on the decisive advertising message. For example, a few years ago the car brand Audi advertised the low fuel consumption of its A6 TDI model. In the commercial, a rental car driver is seen handing the Audi over to a colleague after an extremely long drive with a request for refuelling and no answer to the question "Where is the tank?"

Advertising based on brand sociology is never anti-creative, it just always consistently puts performance at the center of persuasion and does not refer to external trends or supposed changes in values within the clientele. The integration of so-called "benchmarks" always contains a source of danger that puts the specificity of the brand in jeopardy, also with regard to its performance communication to the outside world. The argument often put forward that it is difficult to conduct "performance-oriented communication" because products and services are becoming increasingly similar does not go far enough. Especially when products are becoming more and more similar, it has become a classic (wrong) strategy to look for communication content outside the brand—mostly content that is completely abstract and interchangeable. It is causally illogical to transfer general positive perceptions to a brand: "generality" is the opposite of brand.

What is the brand-sociological alternative? The communicative-promotional work with performance evidence is a sensitive task. It should have become clear that the purely demonstrative presentation of certain facts cannot yet be a strategy, for example the fact that only "best raw materials" are used. The fact that the ingredients are "100% organic" may be interesting, but this information fails to do the job of anchoring a clear image in people's minds. After all, this is how a brand makes itself comparable to the competition.

3.4.4 Reducing Everyday Complexity

In addition, there is the actual task of the brand article for the general public: Its task is to reduce everyday complexity, because brands give us orientation in an increasingly confusing world. Anyone who has consciously stood in front of a yoghurt shelf in a large supermarket can imagine how difficult or impossible it would be to make a decision without any prior brand knowledge. Anyone who has ever been to a McDonald's in India knows that a large number of the customers are Europeans and Americans (also because only this clientele can afford the prices), who look forward to their completely unexcited Big Mac with lettuce leaves and pickles after an adventurous backpacker tour.

> At their core, brands are about knowing what you're going to get. They are "boring" in the best sense of the word and completely "predictable".

This is hardly communicable in times when the cult of the "new" is gladly celebrated in the media, but in the analysis of brand systems, consistency is always a core value. Any performance system that wants to prosper economically in the long term needs a high degree of repetition—no matter how wildly creative or stuffy and conservative the enterprise is. It is precisely this characteristic that saves the purchaser lengthy consideration, scrutiny and, in the final analysis, time. This characteristic alone empowers brands to reduce everyday complexity. What happens when this does not happen is made clear by psychological pathologies: the clinical picture of the autistic person is characterised by the fact that all stimuli have an unfiltered effect on thinking.

Only brands, or the pre-confidence placed in them, make it possible to fill a shopping trolley in the supermarket quasi "blindly" within a few minutes. However, this also means that every brand must deliver its expected performance with absolute consistency down to the last detail and immediately eliminate any deviations. Only those who do not give their customers the opportunity to question the expected performance cultivate blind trust.

Reliability through habit evokes reliability—this is the only way to create attachment, especially in times of abundance.

There are market observers and unfortunately also consultants who postulate the end of "normal" brand strategies and positioning at the expense of any determination: In times in which brands are embedded in an environment of turbulent technical and social change, it is fatal to commit oneself in any form. One runs the risk of no longer being able to react adequately. The opposite is the case, at least for strong, self-confident brands—and these are exactly the ones that are economically successful in the long run: Only those will survive in an ever faster market who show a "clear edge" and present their offer without irritation. As described above, this is not about the slavish identical reproduction of a brand idea, but about the adaptation of the idea within the framework of self-similarity. Less is indeed more (as is so often the case).

3.4.5 Omission as a Virtue

However, this also means: brands must not burden their customers with an excess of information. No customer needs to be informed about the entire organic commitment of Andechser Naturjoghurt (there are probably a myriad of conditions and regulations that the company has installed in the long time of its existence), but the clientele must be able to conclude from a few pieces of information—which are structurally always repeated—that it is a "green product" (design, reference to organic milk and the selected distribution via primarily organic-oriented trade partners). In times of busy schedules and a dramatic-drastic battle for attention through a multitude of signals, it is completely absurd to believe that people want to inform themselves as comprehensively as possible about a brand (unless they are brand fans). It is the task of brand management to identify the actual performance drivers of the brand and to emphasize them again and again—with self-similar variations. Brands reduce complexity. Brands are always specific. Why? Because there is no other way to build trust, which is the basis for the regular inflow of money. This means reflecting on one's core values—every day anew.

Communication that is based solely on proof of performance operates on the surface; it simply gives the customer information. Information may be the basis for a positive relationship, but the main thing is to establish a relationship level between customer and product. This only arises when a few basic attitudes of the brand have solidified, which the customer can accept or reject as such.

Table 3.1 illustrates the operating principle of a brand sociological analysis. This brand characterisation is simple and can be easily memorised (attention: in Table 3.1 only one performance aspect of each of the two brands is shown as an example). In addition, I as an individual can decide for myself whether I share the value attitude associated with the prejudice and can identify with it.

Brands must not overload their clientele with "too much" information out of well-intentioned internal performance orientation and a strong urge to present. Rather, a

Table 3.1 Examples of the operating principle of a brand sociological analysis

Proof of performance/special feature	Prejudice/abstract evaluation
Speick does without chemical additives	Speick is a natural supplier
Wooden radio builds a radio in 16 h handwork	Wooden radio is a high quality product

brand should focus on the decisive contents and thus strengthen the existing bias structure in the sense of a clear orientation and commitment possibility. Insofar as a brand represents values which I claim for myself as desirable and valuable, it functions on the one hand as a possibility of orientation inwardly and at the same time as an object of commitment outwardly, in that I use its statement for my purposes through my purchase and my highly visible use of the brand symbolism, e.g. a certain mineral water stands on the festively laid table. The brand becomes an external mouthpiece of my self-image by making it clear: This is who I am. In the saddest case, this can be a Porsche Cayenne, but also a bottle of "Viva con agua" casually carried through the street. Beverages and luxury foodstuffs in particular offer the opportunity to profess a certain lifestyle relatively inexpensively and yet with a high public profile.

Brands give us the opportunity to define our own personality through their use and commitment to them. After all, strong brands are characterized by the fact that we associate certain attributes with them. A brand like Volvo, for example, has managed to ensure that regardless of whether we are in Germany, Italy, the USA or Japan, the overwhelming majority of people think of attributes such as "safety", "Sweden", "design" and "family" when they hear the name of this brand. An unbelievable achievement: a brand has succeeded in anchoring a global image in people's minds simply by mentioning its name and taking into account that, compared to the existing knowledge, only a few people are drivers of this car. A state of affairs that many an ambitious cultural program of time-honored nations can dream of. The Volvo driver who has chosen precisely this car is aware of this charisma and uses it to make his external image clear with the help of the Volvo. This can happen consciously or subconsciously.

Based on the preceding thoughts, the following "brand-sociological causal chain" emerges:

Brand Sociological Causal Chain

1. Brand is an alliance system.
2. Ideally, alliances take two forms: They are communal or socially based.
3. Brands are communal forms of alliance, products function socially.
4. Brands are to a large extent the return of the same thing over and over again—homologous to the custom in family groups. Expectability arises from performance routine.
5. Man can only build trust with signals that are similar. Because trust is created through familiarity. Trust in a service is at the end of a causal chain:

(continued)

trust only arises when product, form, promise and the overall appearance of a brand are coherent with each other. Only then is a brand believed, it becomes *credible*.

6. By repeatedly broadcasting certain typical performance characteristics to the public, a body of customers forms in the optimal case—i.e. the performance meets with a positive response from the public—which associates certain positively perceived performances with a certain name. This body of customers, which has grown over time, is willing to remain loyal and is therefore insensitive to price (within the framework of the familiar price structure of the brand). The company has succeeded in transforming itself from a marked product into a brand with social symbolic power. The term "customer" makes this point by making it clear that the buyer of a good is "knowledgeable" about the characteristics of that product or service.

7. If certain services are provided under a certain name over time, a positive prejudice about this service(s) is formed. Unlike individual experiences, personal-individual judgments have become socially linked. People have similar experiences independently of each other: A collective judgment has emerged—and the target group extension of this judgment is irrelevant. After all, a solid restaurant only needs to reach its geographical neighbourhood, whereas a globally active company also needs to reach people in Tokyo or New York. In terms of brand sociology, it is not the "size" of the collective judgement that is decisive, but its enforcement in the relevant propensity group.

8. The brand is now in a stable exchange with its environment: it provides services of consistent quality and style. These are perceived, tested and bought if they are liked. Thanks to the repeat buyers, a customer relationship has developed that reduces the testing moment in this group—as long as the brand remains true to itself and acts in a self-similar manner. Besides the fact that the clientele regularly pays money for the service and thus secures the company economically, an immaterial but even higher value is created: the positive prejudice—the basis of every successful brand.

The present chain of effects makes the scientific nature of brand sociology catchy: How brands work and why they are a culture- and world-encompassing phenomenon becomes clear via the derivation from the individual psyche to the collective memory in groups. All stages build on each other. This distinguishes brand sociology from other approaches, which usually only offer solutions at the end of the chain, but disregard the anthropological-cultural dispositions. However, these are the only relevant ones for managing brands effectively.

The summary of contents in Table 3.2 contrasts the brand sociological method with the classical marketing-oriented approach.

Table 3.2 Comparison of brand sociological and marketing-oriented approach

Sociology of brands	Marketing method
Inside oriented	Outside oriented
Identity guided	Image-led
Specifically	Abstract
Consciously	Unconscious
Self-developed	Market research oriented
Perception	Perception
Cause	Effect
Success profile/genetic code	Image analysis

References

Aaker D (1997) Langfristige Markenstrategien. In: Brandmeyer K, Deichsel A (eds) Jahrbuch Markentechnik 1997/98. Deutscher Fachverlag, Frankfurt/Main

Allport GW (1971) Die Natur des Vorurteils. Kiepenheuer & Witsch, Köln

Brandmeyer K (1999) Selbstähnliche Markenführung. Die Gestalt-Gemeinschaft und der Einzelne. In: Kl B, Deichsel A (eds) Jahrbuch Markentechnik. Deutscher Fachverlag, Frankfurt/Main

Bundesministerium der Justiz und für Verbraucherschutz (n.d.) Markenrecht § 3. https://www.gesetze-im-internet.de/markeng/__3.html. Zugegriffen 30. Okt. 2020

Crary J (2014) 24/7. Schlaflos im Spätkapitalismus. Wagenbach, Berlin

Dahm A (2021) PRIMAVERA Bio-Anbaupartnerschaften weltweit – gelebtes Vertrauen. In: Zschiesche A (ed) Vertrauen – die härteste Währung der Welt. Unveröff. Manuskript. Gabal Verlag, Offenbach (in Vorbereitung)

Deichsel A (2006) Markensoziologie. Deutscher Fachverlag, Frankfurt/Main

Deutscher G (2012) Im Spiegel der Sprache. dtv, München

Errichiello O (2021) Gestalt as a determinant of brand management – a sociological perspective on branding in German-Speaking Discourse. J Gestalt Theory 2(2):231–246

Errichiello O, Zschiesche A (2011) Wir Einmaligen. Eichborn, Frankfurt/Main

Errichiello O, Zschiesche A (2013) Markenkraft im Mittelstand. Springer Gabler, Wiesbaden

Esch FR, Wicke A (2001) Herausforderungen und Aufgaben des Markenmanagements. In: Esch FR (ed) Moderne Markenführung, Grundlagen – Innovative Ansätze – Praktische Umsetzungen. Springer Gabler, Wiesbaden

Gabler-Wirtschaftslexikon Band 3 (1997) Springer Gabler, Wiesbaden

Harte-Bavendamm H (2015) Deichsel, die Markentechnik und das Recht. In: Homann T, Zschiesche A, Errichiello O (eds) Die Soziologie, der Gestaltwille und die Marke. Soziale Systeme verstehen und führen. Springer Gabler, Wiesbaden

Haug WF (1971) Kritik der Warenästhetik. Suhrkamp, Frankfurt/Main

Horkheimer M (1962) Über das Vorurteil. In: Arbeitsgemeinschaft für Forschung des Landes Nordrhein-Westfalen (Hrsg) Heft 108. Köln

Kant I (1990) Erste Einleitung in die Kritik der Urteilskraft. Meiner, Hamburg

Kapferer JN (1997) Marke und Ebenbild. In: Unveröffentlichte Konferenzdokumentation des Instituts für Markentechnik Genf zum 1. Internationalen Markentechnikum 1997, Genf

Klein N (2000) No logo. Flamingo, London

Konersmann R (2015) Die Unruhe der Welt. S. Fischer Verlag, Frankfurt/Main

Luhmann N (2000) Vertrauen: Ein Mechanismus der Reduktion sozialer Komplexität. UTB, Stuttgart

Marx K (1973) Das Kapital. Kritik der politischen Ökonomie. Erster Band. Dietz Verlag, Berlin (Ost)

Meffert H (1998) Marketing. Grundlagen marktorientierter Unternehmensführung. Springer Gabler, Wiesbaden

Packard V (1962) Die geheimen Verführer. Der Griff nach dem Unterbewußten in jedermann, Ullstein, Berlin

Pohrt W (2012) Kapitalismus forever. Über Krise, Krieg, Revolution, Evolution, Christentum und Islam. Berlin, Verlag Klaus Bittermann

Pohrt W (2013) Das allerletzte Gefecht. Über den universellen Kapitalismus, den Kommunismus als Episode und die Menschheit als Amöbe, den Kommunismus als Episode und die Menschheit als Amöbe. Verlag Klaus Bittermann, Berlin

Pschera A (2011) 800 Millionen. Apologie der sozialen Medien. Matthes & Seitz, Berlin

Readers Digest: Most Trusted Brands (2019). https://www.horizont.net/marketing/nachrichten/trusted-brands-studie-das-sind-die-vertrauenswuerdigsten-marken-und-medien-der-deutschen-173964. Zugegriffen Aug 2020

Rosa H (2005) Die Veränderung der Zeitstrukturen in der Moderne. Suhrkamp, Frankfurt/Main

Schmoll T, Winkelmann M (2015) Grüne Propaganda. In: enorm 05/2015, Hamburg

Sombart W (1908) Die Reklame. In: Der Morgen 06.03.1908, Berlin

Twenge JM, Campbell WK (2010) The narcissism epidemic. Living in the age of entitlement. Simon & Schuster, New York

von Weizsäcker CC (2001) Vertrauen als Koordinationsmechanismus. In: Brandmeyer K, Deichsel A, Prill C (eds) Jahrbuch Markentechnik 2002/2003. Deutscher Fachverlag, Frankfurt/Main

Waldrop MM (1993) Inseln im chaos. Die Erforschung komplexer Systeme. Rohwolt, Reinbek

Williams R (1961) Advertising: the magic system. In: Problems in materialism and culture. Verso, London

Winkelmann M (2013) Überholtes Modell. Interview mit Pavan Sukhdev. In: enorm: 05/2013, Hamburg

Zernisch P (2003) Markenglauben managen. Eine Markenstrategie für Unternehmer. Weinheim, Wiley-VCH Verlag

Zschiesche A, Errichiello O (2009) Erfolgsgeheimnis Ost: Survival-Strategien der besten Marken – und was Manager daraus lernen können. Springer Gabler, Wiesbaden

Development, Evolution and Management of a Green Brand

4

Abstract

In this chapter, the "wooden radio" project, one of the most successful global eco-design projects, is described in a catchy way and the "genetic code" of the brand, i.e. the success profile, is analysed and operationalised as an example. The success profile, one of the most common brand management tools, identifies all the characteristics that a company has typically delivered over time. These causes can be specifically controlled by the company management. Future strategic decisions in the areas of brand development, brand building, brand architecture are thus given a scientifically sound basis and safeguarding. Building on this, project descriptions and instructions for action on the success profile of the brand provide an overview of how an existing brand can be built up and controlled in a planned manner or how new brands follow a highly individual construction plan.

4.1 Green Brand Management Using the Example of Wooden Radio

4.1.1 Initial Situation

In 1971, the designer Victor Papanek wrote down his design credo in a thin booklet entitled "Design for the Real World". He stated, "There are professions that do more harm than that of the industrial designer, but many are not." (Papanek 2014, p. 20). Papanek's reasoning is understandable against the background that green design hardly played a role until a few years ago. Especially brands that are considered design trendsetters are not usually associated with ecology or fair production methods. For this reason, the "David Report", a thesis paper by product designers David Carlson and Brent Richards, still formulates 50 years after Papanek's thoughts: "Lets face it; design is now a major source of pollution, as process and a phenomenon, design has degenerated into a state of aesthetic proliferation that has

© Springer Fachmedien Wiesbaden GmbH, part of Springer Nature 2022
O. Errichiello, A. Zschiesche, *Green Branding*,
https://doi.org/10.1007/978-3-658-36060-3_4

accumulative and destructive levels, in terms or flow of meaning, value, and identity." (Carlson and Richards 2010). A qualitative evolution of design is only possible with a changed self-image: "The diagnosis is not making design better, but making design matter.[...] Design is no longer about the lifestyle, but the lifecycle. [...] What makes us want to retain and keep certain objects (however worn and bettered) while we throw others away without thinking twice about it? Is there a lesson to be learned, and is there a useable formula for making design matter more? [...] We need new storytellers." (Carlson and Richards 2010). This insight has given rise to the notion of sustainable design, or ecodesign, over the last decade.

What is understood by Ecodesign? The following definition can be found on the website of the "Ecodesign Preis Deutschland":

> The term 'EcoDesign' describes a systematic approach that aims to integrate ecological aspects into the product planning, development and design process as early as possible. This means that the requirement of 'environment' is added to the classic criteria of product development such as economy, safety, reliability, ergonomics, technical feasibility and last but not least aesthetics. The term EcoDesign expresses that ecology and economy are to be united within the EcoDesign approach with the help of good design. In short, EcoDesign leads to products, systems, infrastructures, and services that require a minimal amount of resources, energy, and space while optimally fulfilling the desired benefits, while minimizing pollutant use and emissions and waste—throughout the entire product life cycle. (Cf. Tischner et al. 2000, p. 12).

Wooden radio implemented these principles at a time when there were still no definitions and awards, and thus introduced a new understanding of products in an exemplary manner. All the more astonishing because the underlying understanding of product and sustainability was not the result of a Western "think tank", but rather arose from the experience and life of the "local inventor", who had no part in any of the usual designer networks.

4.1.2 New Craft: The History of Wooden Radio

The wooden radio is the idea and the product of the Indonesian designer Singgih Susilo Kartono, who studied design at the University of Bandung in the 1980s and was then faced with the question of whether he should work as a salaried designer for a local furniture company (cf. Fig. 4.1). Kartono decided against a permanent position and set up his own production in his home village of Kandangan (Temanggung district), about 500 km south of the city of Yogyakarta. This decision was not to be expected, since Kandangan, in contrast to other parts of Indonesia, is not characterized by a significant "production culture of furniture or accessories", but rather by an agricultural character.

During his studies, he rarely had the opportunity to travel to his homeland due to limited financial resources, but it was precisely over the longer intervals between his visits that he noticed the changes in his region: forced by government programmes,

Fig. 4.1 From the village to the metropolis: Singgih Susilo Kartono and the "Magno wooden radio". (Courtesy of © Errichiello/Zschiesche gbr (wooden radio) 2020. All Rights Reserved)

farmers were urged to adopt "rapid modernisation measures" and abandon traditional methods of farming in return. The artificial "strengthening" of the soil through chemical fertilizers and genetically modified seeds changed agriculture and had a negative impact on working methods, operations and ultimately the entire village community. Jobs were increasingly lost. Many residents left the village and moved to surrounding towns as factory workers. It became clear to Kartono that the "modern forms" of agriculture were not able to consolidate his village as a functioning community. Could design help stabilize the village social microsystem? Kartono's goal: Through contemporary handicraft products, the village should once again be a serious option as a place to live and work for all generations (cf. Fig. 4.2).

During his studies Kartono learned from the Indonesian artist and designer Surya Pernawa. Pernawa developed the "New Craft" method, according to which, in contrast to traditional forms of "folkloric design", it is not a matter of *a* craftsman making a product (the craftsman takes care of all production stages/parts of the product), but of dividing production into different stages and operationalizing and organizing these design areas to individual specialists. In this way, manufacturing know-how is quickly acquired and larger quantities can be produced in short time intervals—at the same time, although the products are handmade, the range of variation in terms of processing is limited. A retailer always gets a *marginally* different variant of a product.

The new craft methodology has many advantages: it allows the creation of innovative economic activities in areas that are not characterized by any craft culture. At the same time, both existing and "dying" craft businesses can be successfully revitalized. The result of new craft is handcrafted goods that meet consistent quality

Fig. 4.2 Cradle of wooden radio: team and production site. (Courtesy of © Errichiello/Zschiesche gbr (wooden radio) 2020. All Rights Reserved)

standards. Handmade products are given a contemporary definition with new craft: instead of folkloric design, the design language is based on a professional and contemporary production and design concept. The ideas of design are brought into harmony with manufacturing requirements in a controlled process, thus enabling value-added marketing.

For Kartono, design does not mean developing a finished product at a desk and implementing it in the workshop. As he himself puts it, "For me, designing means acting without a map." He strictly rejects market studies. Rather, it's about recognizing relevance in the process of trying things out for oneself, which ultimately flows into a product. Precisely because products must never claim to be perfect, Kartono works primarily with the "imperfect" material wood, which does not adhere to exact standards in terms of texture and colour. Basically, he tries to change the relationship between object and human being through his products. It should no longer be about mere functioning, but about the challenge of making the product as an object experienceable again by placing a special emphasis on details. The name Magno (for "magnify") refers to his desire to make details recognizable again. For example, the wooden radio does without a transmitter scale, so that the user is forced to deal with the object.

4.1.3 Brand Development of Wooden Radio

Kartono started making wooden children's toys in the early 2000s—initial experience that was useful for him to start producing the first wooden radio in 2005—as a one-man operation in the children's room of a rented house (see Fig. 4.3).

Fig. 4.3 Individual instead of mass production. (Courtesy of © Errichiello/Zschiesche gbr (wooden radio) 2020. All Rights Reserved)

A chance encounter led him to success, but above all to a longstanding, mutually inspiring intercontinental cooperation between Indonesia and Europe: In 2006, I, Oliver Errichiello, was the marketing manager of a German garden furniture manufacturer and in this capacity visited the Jakarta Fair, a kind of international performance show of Indonesian companies. This fair hardly differs from the typical consumer fairs of this world: companies outbid each other with high quality standards, a good price-performance ratio, short delivery times, flexible production capacities. Visitors are given tickets to hang around their necks, with the word "Buyer" written unmistakably on them. If you stop for just a moment at one of the hundreds of stands, the staff there will be overflowing with devout friendliness in an attempt to win over the European or American trader. An attitude that far too often brings with it an inadequate behaviour on the part of Western buyers: Economic colonialism of the new age. In the midst of this mass-market oriented fair, between the spatially enormous presences of the manufacturers, two small shelves hardly stand out. The exhibitor here was the Indonesian government, which gives small businesses the opportunity to show their wares in a modest pavilion. On the shelves were radios that stood out in the monotony of standardized design language: They defied established aesthetics and had an independent design. Quite in contrast to the other stands, not a single salesman came directly "to help". I was left to look at the radios undisturbed, until finally my uncertain turning around and looking for someone to talk to led to a shy man approaching me. We chatted amiably, I was allowed to

102   4 Development, Evolution and Management of a Green Brand

touch the radio and operate its knobs and switches—and wanted to buy one immediately. The man turned out to be the designer and producer of the radios, Singgih Susilo Kartono, and . . . categorically refused my request to buy: these radios were his life's work, the result of a years-long process of discovery, and were meant to safeguard the viability of his village. Unusual statements in a place where reality provides only quick reactions and answers—and a refusal to sell is the most absurd thing a buyer can imagine. There, where it is otherwise about "money, profit and margin", now a supplier first talks about "community". Before selling, he wanted to get to know me first, after all, one does not give "one's baby" to just anyone for free use. The radio, he said, was merely a vehicle for the questions of people's relationship to their products and at the same time the key to the question of how small, remote villages could be made viable again for young people. Irritation on my part, a smile on the part of this odd person in the middle of a sales fair. We exchanged email addresses and went back to our two normal lives.

Often first meetings have the peculiarity of anticipating the basic style of a relationship: It was clear that this was not a producer hoping for the quick deal despite an outstanding offer, but this was about understanding people in a special life situation. A few months after the meeting in Jakarta, Kartono's address fell into my hands again and I wrote my first email: "Dear Singgih, please tell me more about your village—Best wishes, Oliver". The answer came promptly.

What followed was a year of discussion and lively email exchanges between a small Javanese village and Hamburg—a time that was good and helpful in understanding why such a special radio was created in a region that is otherwise mostly associated with mass production at the expense of people and the environment. Kartono in turn learned that our profession as socio-economists is the scientifically based management of brands. The underlying ethical-commercial understanding of brands and services was a perfect match for his aspiration to distribute and sell his wooden radio. Thus the idea arose to jointly win the European market for an Indonesian wooden radio. The naive start: Without a written contract, without a business plan, but only through the communication of a story and an outstanding design performance behind it, we wanted to bring this unique product to Europe. The first delivery of 48 wooden radios reached the port of Hamburg on July 18, 2007 (see Fig. 4.4).

Fig. 4.4 The original model: Magno wooden radio wr01a-2bipod. (Courtesy of © Errichiello/Zschiesche gbr (wooden radio) 2020. All Rights Reserved)

The initial situation seemed hopeless: No one needed a hand-built analogue radio made of wood for 179 € in 2007. Because at the same time, Internet radios were becoming increasingly common. High-fidelity sound even from small radios became a matter of course, and digital radio receivers became the standard. At first glance, there was no prospect of commercial success—and pity buys are very rarely a viable long-term business proposition. There was also no distribution network, and we had no advertising budget to work with at the time. On the contrary, we first had to pass various testings to even launch the radio into the European market, as well as factor in annual costs to comply with electrical and equipment regulations. Therefore, the initial focus was on informing people about the radio and its background idea, as well as its special origin, and using this story to target possible media multipliers— informing various newspapers and magazines. First articles also appear in international design blogs and report about a wooden radio from Java. We receive the first inquiries.

The first task was to find regional shops that were willing to offer this radio to their customers. Trend-setting shops were the first port of call for peddling the radio: We criss-crossed Hamburg by car, looked for suitable businesses and then tried to make appointments on the spot with the managers or those responsible for the area. After all, the presence of the radio in the specialist shops was to be an important further strategic step, so that people would automatically "talk about a unique radio". In order to specifically win over national specialist dealers as sales partners, trade fair appearances had to follow: In 2008, wooden radio exhibited for the first time at the "ambiente" and "tendence" consumer goods trade fairs in Frankfurt. The usual "green" trade fairs were dispensed with and instead a presence was shown at emphatically high-consumption trade fairs. The radio and the booth attracted attention: In doing so, we allowed ourselves a trick of necessity and booked "remaining space" with the trade fair organisers, who recognised the special nature of the project (and also used it to their advantage). The smallest stand of the fair (4 m^2) was unique not only because of the radio. In 2009, trade fair appearances followed in Berlin, Paris, Milan, Stockholm, Copenhagen and London. In total, wooden radio had 15 national and European trade fair presences from 2008 to 2014. In the monotony of the large trade suppliers and manufacturers, the product not only attracted the attention of dealers looking for special features, but also defied the industry's own rules: for example, the restriction of production to 300 to 600 (varying annual production) wooden radios per month set by Singgih Kartono leads to the introduction of waiting lists for dealers. All "our" dealers were always reminded of their responsibility towards the project as a whole, with the urgent request not to make drastic price reductions on the basis of short-term considerations (cf. Figs. 4.5 and 4.6).

In 2009, the rise of the brand began: A 10-min TV report at prime time brought the breakthrough. Suddenly wooden radio was known all over Germany. We had to interrupt our holidays to take wooden-radio orders by phone and pack packages all day long. We had to inform many of those who were willing to buy about a waiting period of at least 2 months, there was not a single protest, everyone showed understanding. Weekly reports on the radio in European media as well as the

Fig. 4.5 Trade fairs with message: ambiente consumer goods trade fair, 2012. (Courtesy of © Errichiello/Zschiesche gbr (wooden radio) 2020. All Rights Reserved)

Fig. 4.6 Mega poster at the Paris trade fair stand—Brand is border. (Courtesy of © Errichiello/Zschiesche gbr (wooden radio) 2020. All Rights Reserved)

penetration of the markets through presence in upscale design and furniture stores led to a permanent and steadily growing demand. At its peak (2010 to 2012), the waiting time for a wooden radio was 6 months. The strongest markets are Germany (approx. 50% of sales), Italy (20%), Austria (10%) as well as Denmark, BENELUX, France and Great Britain (see Fig. 4.7). The proceeds were used to finance an exemplary production facility, which also includes seminar and social rooms for

Fig. 4.7 Wooden radio radios 2012. (Courtesy of © Errichiello/Zschiesche gbr (wooden radio) 2020. All Rights Reserved).

the village community. At the same time, we started a tree planting programme with the local high school: the students plant tree seeds, grow them and finally hand them over to the company's own nursery for rearing, which eventually spreads the small trees around the village in a village-wide planting campaign.

Until 2013, the great demand continued due to the diverse media coverage, then it slowly became quieter. Dedicated dealers continue to sell the wooden radio persistently and with high commitment.

In 2015, the brand activity finally underwent a future-proof change: although the "wooden radio" has become a global eco-design icon, the lower demand due to the organic product life cycle made it difficult to cover the costs of international distribution: Singgih Kartono continues to produce wooden radios, but distributes them primarily through design shops in Indonesia and the country's tourist centres. The focus will now be on communicating the production and sales experience for "green production in the sense of the New Craft". Singgih Kartono believes that "Craft is an alternative economic activity that has the potential to be developed and to grow in villages. It has characteristics that are suitable for villages' living conditions and growth prospects. These characteristics are that it is labor intensive, requires low technology and investment and abundance of local material input."

(Dunn 2016). Through seminars and training, designers and entrepreneurs learn about this form of local business. The proceeds of the wooden radio go directly into the conversion of large areas of land into organic agriculture and fish farming, as well as the development of nature-based tourism.

In 2014, Kartono held its first international conference on this topic, "The 1st International Conference on Village Revitalization", in its home village, and introduced another product to strengthen economic sustainability: The "Spedagi Bamboo Bicycle". Kartono elaborates:

> The bamboo bicycle was created to be a conversation-starter about a sustainable design movement. While of course it is still a real product made by Indonesians for the local market, the purpose was never to focus solely on production of bamboo bicycles—there are many international companies already making bicycles out of alternative materials. The Spedagi is a way of showcasing local Indonesian design potential that doesn't rely on the export market for economic survival—as is mostly the case with Magno wooden products. Kartono's intentions also link to eco-tourism ambitions for the village. It is hoped that the bamboo bicycle acts as a magnet to draw people to the village, inviting curiosity, as well as being a handy method of transportation for visitors and volunteers who stay in the guesthouses. (Dunn 2016).

Thus wooden radio serves as a supporting element for the ecosocial change processes on a local level and as a worldwide example project far beyond a product.

4.2   The Success Profile of Green Brands Using the Example of Wooden Radio

What can be learned from the brief description of the "wooden radio" brand for managing a brand in day-to-day business? First and foremost, that the specificity of a brand can only ever emerge from within itself, from its individual history. If brand is a positive prejudice, which is created by the daily redemption of expected performances, then a substantial statement about the core values of the brand can only be made, if the causes for this image are decidedly present. This means that a value creation-oriented brand analysis must begin with the observation of the first day.

If you look at the development of the company and the brand wooden radio over time, you will see that certain characteristics and service contents have remained almost the same—despite changing framework and market conditions. They also form the basis for the planned further development of the company today. They provide the system of coordinates in which the brand must act, if it wants to anchor the positive prejudice regarding its name more deeply, in order to strengthen the value creation power in a targeted manner.

As described before: Brand sociological analysis takes the impact level (image) as a starting point to isolate the causes of this external image in the internal actions of the company. Specifically:

- What are the reasons why many people today attribute a high level of competence in the field of natural skin care to the "Dr. Hauschka" brand? Even people who have never bought a Dr. Hauschka product.
- What are the reasons why the soft drink Lemonaid is perceived as a hip, young product and drunk with a clear conscience?
- What are the reasons that a hand-built radio made of wood, still equipped with a simple analog receiver in times of high-fidelity sound, can still be sold all over Europe at a premium price?

The decisive factor is that the structural pattern—the organic blueprint of brand bodies—is never open: Unlike a machine blueprint, the blueprint of a brand as a living system is highly complex and lived primarily by people who, while at best developing a "feel" for the brand, do not robotically work off that feel. This is because the genetics of a brand, while recognizable in numerous variations at every contact, are not mapped anywhere. This makes analysis difficult: intuitive expressions of feeling about a brand ("I believe that this brand stands for quality/innovation/etc.") must in fact all be traced back to their concrete causes. Only through precise and far-reaching observation can these success-giving structural patterns within the system be identified. With the help of long-term observation, repetitive interactions between brand and people, but also between the individual people themselves, become recognizable. It becomes clear in which areas they form the specific brand system. The decisive performance content of a brand, its substance, can be worked out through the brand's success profile and operationalized for brand management.

The success profile eludes the flood of new as well as revitalized old approaches and models because it is not a model in the conventional sense. Because the success profile does not derive its content from "new insights", but it is a logical causal model of cause and effect. Thus, the brand sociological analysis of a brand is not a magic craft, a management fashion from the magnetic resonance tomographs of this world (see neuromarketing) or the marketing idea of a whacky trend guru who propagates a new consumer image.

▶ **It's Simple**
   A brand is characterized by specific achievements and peculiarities, which together form a specific system code. This "genetic code", the success profile, guides the evolution of a brand.

The analogy of organic living beings (humans, animals, plants) and ideal living beings (e.g. brands) was pointed out by the French economist Jean-Noel Kapferer as early as the 1990s when he wrote: "The genetic analogy lies in the understanding of the brand. The storehouse of information carries within it the program of future developments, the particular attributes of future types of products, their commonalities and similarities that link the individual products in the portfolio." (Kapferer 1992, p. 50).

The success profile of the brand characterizes that the decisive building blocks of success of the company are determined and made accessible to the brand management. The objective is clear: the success profile is intended to uncover the pattern of action that has conditioned the success of the company, based on the convincing performance from the past to the present. In effect, the success profile is the analytical basis for cultivating the existential reasons for success and thus the cause for maximum value creation—an action instruction for steering a social body.

> The fundamental question in the analysis of the success profile is: What specific performance contexts have made the brand successful and anchored it in people's minds?

With recourse to the brand-sociological functional chain of brands, this question must be brought into focus because only a successful performance is reproduced by a system. This is logical: brands can only reproduce what brings them something economically. In the long run, no system can afford to undertake things that are not worthwhile and do not generate an economic response or clientele. Naturally, a brand and its services must constantly seek resonance and thus success. Research into the sociology of brands has established that brands still have a high degree of freedom at the beginning of their development: Starting from a performance idea, a brand tries itself out, sometimes adopts highly different strategies, since it still has to find its success profile first. This works until it finally meets with approval and generates sales with a certain product and an individual form of marketing—or it fades away. However, once the brand has resonated, it remains true to this successful system; after all, the pattern has brought it the success it hoped for. Changes now take place more and more cautiously as time goes on—nothing should upset the existing success profile, shake the trust that has been painstakingly built up. A brand has been created. In short:

> A brand is also characterized above all by the integration of system-maintaining mutation blockades: the drawing of boundaries.

With the success profile, a clear picture emerges of which services are decisive for the brand, which must be further developed in the future in a self-similar manner and which attributes are not up for disposal.

Experience shows that some building blocks of success have existed since the foundation of a company, others only became part of the success profile through trial and error—as a living system, the brand constantly integrates new aspects and sorts out unsuccessful performance components. What is important in the analytical consideration of brands is that a brand never has its purpose in itself, it is always a means to an end: brands are not bought by people because they are brands (even Prada must *factually* correspond to the high quality or trend-setting character of the brand), but always because they offer a certain form of performance and attitude. While the impulse to buy a branded good may well be psychologically based (the prestige of the good name is supposed to radiate to the buyer), even such a buyer will examine whether the brand's performance matches its claim to value. To put it succinctly:

Image alone does not sell image.

Against this background, a company must not only stand for and communicate certain values, but it is the special challenge to make these values operationalizable and concrete.

As mentioned before, brands are very often described with so-called image categories. What they all have in common is the fact that brands are supposed to be defined here on the basis of general, abstract and mostly open to interpretation terms. In the case of large companies, intensive market research is added to this: these are often statements about the brand made by customers or even randomly selected persons, which have been collected in the course of surveys or market research studies. These results pose problems that are dangerous to the brand, because:

- **Abstractions** never describe realities. Abstractions do not occur in life. At best, they suggest a definition. No one talks about having enjoyed a particularly "close to nature" holiday. Instead, he will talk about the vegetables from the organic hotel's own garden or about the solar system on the roof, the homemade jam, the "cute donkeys" on the farm grounds. The Italian organic farm and organic food mail order company "La Viala" breaks all the usual rules in its internet presence: The font is a barely legible cursive, the image division barely allows perception, the texts are endless . . . and yet: the brand is considered highly successful and its products are part of many pantries of ecology-minded headmasters. Communication always happens concretely, only—contrary to all life experience—many people in marketing are used to starting from abstract facts. (The brand has maintained this form of design across all channels and product designs for many years without irritation).
- **Images** are always effects of long-term actions of the company. In contrast to actions, however, image effects cannot be controlled, i.e. they cannot be operationalized by the brand manager. No company manager can explicitly control which emotional worlds are to be experienced by his customers. Images are useless for the management of a brand. What exactly is meant by quality can be discussed for days in meetings without a sufficient solution. What a high quality standard is will be defined differently in Swabia than in Dublin or even in the USA. For an organic farm with a farm shop, quality means something completely different than it does for an ecological electricity provider. What is a definition worth if it does not provide unambiguity and thus does not make clear what a brand stands for?

The winners of such a "logic" are not the brands, but only those providers who live from brands or their consulting. The focus on abstract brand definitions provides market research service providers and advertising agencies with a profitable business model. Abstract brand definitions allow the development of "standard recipes" that can easily be adapted to any client. However, brands are highly individual and—analogous to custom—have their justifications within themselves. Recipes and strategies that apply to one company are completely useless for another. Assuming this, it can only be decided whether a campaign or advertisement helps a company if the reasons for its success are concretely available.

> Pointing to the competition gives management an apparent "fact-based" argument for their own decision: "If someone else did it, it can't be bad."

In order to circumvent the weaknesses of classic brand management, a brand analysis based on brand sociology works exclusively with real, tangible services that are provided under a name. Only sensually perceptible elements and interactions that are "typical" for the brand over time are recorded. They are the characteristics that describe the collective memory and evaluation of a brand. The decisive point is: brand systems are always formed by several success components.

The value creation staircase, in the sense of a qualitative enrichment at each stage—as opposed to the concept of a value chain—must be worked out. In doing so, the analysis of the success profile is not limited to the usual marketing instruments (i.e. marketing mix), but encompasses all areas that can be experienced by the clientele in a direct or indirect manner. This includes, for example, research and development, production, sales, distribution and customer service. This is because the following questions cannot be answered with an analysis of the "advertising role", although they are crucial for the perception of the brand:

- How has the company performed and in what ways from the day it was founded until today?
- What was "typically" reproduced in these areas?
- What could not prevail and describes the limits of the brand?

Every living system unfolds an individual success profile. Based on its stylistics, each brand system produces something unique, because all (exchangeable) information, raw materials, services and processing methods are integrated, interpreted and finally realized.

With the success profile of the brand, an instrument is available with which the brand manager can build up (his) brand in a targeted manner. The given path is not a wishful thinking, not an idealization in the sense of a "so-would-we-like". Rather, the material for the development of a brand is located solely within the company itself. This approach has advantages:

1. Brand management is based on verifiable facts.
2. Brand management can only focus on the content that is actually delivered—no chance for green washing.

3. Internal discussions on the basis of gut instinct or judgements of likeability are no longer necessary, because the assessment of whether a product or an advertisement is "coherent" must be proven solely by the success profile.

In the following, using the example of the brand wooden radio, it will be explained on the basis of clear work steps how the "success profile of a brand" can be worked out and how this analytical work directly influences the day-to-day business and in effect causes a positive added value of the company. This analysis structure fulfils the objective of working out the genetic code of a brand and has proven itself as a methodology for over 30 years in more than 500 companies.

4.2.1   Step 1 to Strengthen Value Creation: How to Organise an Analysis of the Success Profile?

The project organization plays an outstanding role in the analysis of the brand's success profile. In addition to analytical questions, the psychological dispositions of those involved must also be taken into account. This is because a brand sociological analysis deals with intuitive know-how and attempts to identify overarching structural patterns in individuals in relation to a company. If at the end of an analysis process binding structures are defined for each individual employee, it is crucial to involve as many of these people as possible in the process of elaboration and to ask them for their knowledge. This has two advantages: On the one hand, one deals with the long-maintained performance content of the brand, and on the other hand, one integrates as many employees as possible into the analysis. This approach prevents the results from being perceived as "imposed" and helps with acceptance when it comes to implementation. In order to fulfill this premise, the analysis process should be structured as follows:

> **Success Profile: Structure of the Analysis Process**
> 1. **Group analytical interview**
>   In a one-day group retreat, all department heads or important (and long-standing) top performers meet. In a moderated discussion, the individual departments are asked in detail about their performance history and content development as well as their special features. A detailed questionnaire was sent to the participants about 2 weeks beforehand. In the interview, the aim is not to work through event-related, form-filling PowerPoint presentations, but to find out about the decisive milestones and work processes of the departments in discussions. Short presentations can introduce the topics. The information obtained is documented. Audio or film recordings should be avoided for psychological reasons.

(continued)

Caution: In some companies, it has proven useful for the flow of information to forego the presence of the head of the company. The risk is too great that the participants report selectively or omit internal difficulties. The decision for such an approach must be made internally. It is conceivable at such a kick-off meeting to integrate employees who have already retired. As a rule, they contribute a lot to making the development of a company comprehensible—and a positive signal is sent internally: Experience counts at our company.

2. **Individual interviews/on-site company investigation**

   Based on the information previously obtained in the group interview, individual participants are interviewed again in interviews lasting approximately 1 h. If necessary, the management will now also be integrated. The statements made by the participants are discussed in depth. In addition, research visits are made to the company or to the interfaces with the clientele, including shops, call centres, warehouses, sales trips, training courses, ritualised events/celebrations for the clientele. These areas in particular are critical to fully understanding the genetics of a company. The results are documented.

3. **Analysis phase**

   Handed over documents (business management evaluations, old sales documents, advertising materials, etc.) are evaluated and brought into connection with the statements of the group and individual interviews. The brand sociological analysis is applied. On the basis of the available information material, recurring patterns and "typical" structures within the brand are obtained. The result is the "success profile of the brand" with its success modules and performance components.

4. **Fact check**

   The developed success building blocks of the brand as well as its constituent components/services are checked for correctness before the presentation.

5. **Presentation to a small circle**

   The brand's success profile is presented to the management, any strategic corrections are integrated, and initial general recommendations are discussed in a small circle. Based on the success profile, recommendations can be made with regard to all examined performance fields and departments. Deviations and undesirable developments from the brand's genetics are named.

6. **Presentation in front of a larger circle**

   The employees surveyed in the group interview learn the results of the study. In the optimal case, the management announces its brand strategy on the basis of the results or presents the individual success components and derives the strategic course settings for the employees in an understandable way.

The pivotal point of the analysis is the history with the concrete performance contents and the resulting unique characteristics of the brand. At first glance, it is completely irrelevant whether individual performance characteristics are also provided identically by competitors, since only the totality of all characteristics determines the overall shape of the brand. If you look at a brand like wooden radio, the material "wood" will certainly also be a performance feature of other radio providers, but it is only from the multitude of different building blocks (as a rule, each brand has 8–12 success building blocks) that the unique brand emerges.

4.2.2   Step 2 to Strengthen Value Creation: Where and What to Look for to Determine the Success Profile of the Brand?

After the organizational grid in which the investigation takes place has been set, it is necessary to precisely determine research content and its operationalizability: The isolation of the "brand success profile" is based, on the one hand, on a sound factual knowledge of the subject under investigation and, more importantly, on its arrangement and condensation in terms of the sociology of brands. Sociology as a doctrine dealing with collective patterns and forces of attraction draws on this learnable pattern sensitivity. In our 20 years of brand activity, we have developed the know-how to recognize these patterns. Again and again we find that the exact differentiation between image, building block of success and component in the company does not succeed at first go. The brand sociologist also needs constant self-examination in a dialogical discovery process in order to make the contents of a brand operable. What mayhelp is a

- dedicated questionnaire and
- a clear structuring of the performance fields of a brand.

On the basis of the performance territory of a brand and its fields of action, essential questions for the analysis of the company can be formulated. Where to look for a brand sociological analysis?

Brand Action Fields
In contrast to a classic marketing-oriented strategy, a brand sociological brand analysis is not limited to the classic fields of action of advertising, communication and PR. For many brands, these areas only play a subordinate role. On the other hand, it is important to operationalize all areas that can be directly experienced by the customer. Because a customer does not differentiate between intended and unintended communication when coming into contact with a brand. Everything that is provided under the umbrella of a brand is composed by the human being into a gestalt: The personal experience with a salesperson of the brand, his clothes (suit or polo shirt), the ambience at the place of sale, the condition of the delivery trucks, the expression of the employees in the call center create the image in our minds. Against this background, it is not only negligent but simply wrong to limit oneself to classic

marketing fields. The organizational restrictions are internal demarcation mechanisms that have nothing to do with brand reality.

The structuring on the basis of five fields of action clarifies the design context around a performance idea. In interaction, the fields form a performance body that orders and shapes the stylistics of the individual areas. The following five dimensions usually depict the performance of a brand:

1. Product
2. Advertising/Communication
3. Population
4. Distribution
5. Management

1. **Dimension: Product**

The product or service is nothing more than the realization of the actual brand idea. Behind every product there is initially the impulse of a founder, a powerful "I want this to be so", which offers a specific solution to a problem that does not yet exist.[1] Sometimes these are "ingenious inventions" (iphone), sometimes it is just a focus within an existing service system (delivery within 24 h), although a "just" can sometimes be the decisive competitive advantage.

The (original) brand idea is in many cases—in a self-similar variant—still the core benefit of a brand today. For example, the fashion company C&A entered its founding phase from 1841 in the Netherlands (Germany in 1911) with the objective of "offering quality fashion at a reasonable price"—this is now well over 100 years Wooden radio has combined a technical product with traditional manufacturing methods. This aspect will always play a role in the planned further development of the brand and the question of new products. It cumulates in the statement: If wooden radio offers a product, then not only an outstanding design is sufficient, but the design must integrate modern electronics with craftsmanship.

Over time, there is usually a differentiation of the offer of a brand: The assortment is expanded in order to address new customer groups or to offer even more individual product solutions. However, even an ill-considered line extender that does not meet the original brand idea can violate the self-similar brand structure—and thus unsettle the clientele. Therefore, the following questions arise for the questionnaire of the analysis with regard to the *product field of action:*

---

[1]However, this serious long-term starting point of an entrepreneurial activity is sometimes threatened in times of business start-ups. Occasionally, one has the impression that many young (Internet-based) companies are founded in order to collect as much "venture capital" as quickly as possible and to pursue a so-called "exit strategy". No wonder that so far only a few companies of the New Economy have proven that they are brands and not just business concepts.

Questionnaire on the Product Field of Action
- What was the founding idea of the brand?
- Were there any special/unique methods/techniques?
- What was the initial response to the founding products? Why?
- Is the product/service limited to one idea or has it already developed offshoots?f
- What products/services failed to catch on within the story?
- How original is the product in its segment compared to competitors?
- If available: How important is the area of research & development? Which products were developed or invented here?
- Is the product associated with special personalities and discoveries?
- How is purchasing organized? Are there special rules and principles? If so, which ones?

2. **Dimension: Advertising/communication**

If it is a question of constantly anchoring a uniform image, i.e. a positive preconception, in the audience in the long term, advertising must exhibit a high degree of self-similarity. Constant changes in style and the technical adaptation of advertising to target groups make it difficult to form a uniform image of the product or service which, after all, is the brand in the first place. Hans Domizlaff, the founder of the brand technique, a European form of gaining entrepreneurial trust, wrote in his work "Die Gewinnung des öffentlichen Vertrauens -Ein Lehrbuch der Markentechnik" (The Gaining of Public Trust—A Textbook of Brand Technique), which was first published in 1939 and has become a classic: "It is not advertising that should become conscious, but brand trust that should be strengthened subconsciously." (Domizlaff 2005, p. 111). For wooden radio, the original product is always the focus of communication and is the visual anchor point for being associated with a certain "product"—even if far more products enrich the portfolio in the meantime. The slogan "It takes 16 h to create a fine radio" will continue to be a central communication content. This slogan allows variations within the framework of self-similarity, as long as the actual message—"manual work" and thus the connection to "value" anchored in the collective memory—is retained, for example in the case of the wooden radio desk set: "It takes 3 h to create a fine desktop set.

With regard to the *field of action advertising/communication, the* following contents result for the questionnaire of the analysis:

Questionnaire for the Field of Action Advertising/Communication
- What did the company's first advertisements look like? Letters/ prospectuses that do not fall within the scope of classic advertising but list initial arguments/ideas can also be examined.
- What is the style of the advertising/PR? What is the evolution over time (design, language, arguments, color, motifs, etc.)?
- Which advertising media are used and to what extent?
- Where and when is advertising (historical/current)?
- Who is the advertising/PR aimed at (historically/currently)?
- Are there any outstanding motifs, slogans or events since the foundation?
- Are there any incidents/performances that have attracted special attention in our audience (this does not necessarily have to have been a classic advertising medium)?

3. **Dimension: Population**

A brand is only a brand when a uniform, stable idea about certain characteristics exists in the market. Without the knowledge of the history behind it, a Mercedes star would only be an abstract sign showing three long prongs in a closed circle. Only a directed, collective prejudice makes a brand recognizable as well as calculable and in the long run considerably lowers the efforts of persuasion. For this reason, a twofold analysis is necessary when assessing whether a brand is strong or weak: on the one hand, the typological composition of the brand community (its social mix) should be fathomed, and on the other hand, the brand public should be treated on the basis of structural analytical data. This is primarily important for group brands because internal structures often demand this kind of double safeguarding.

Brand sociology describes the density levels of a brand public via the so-called 4-C scheme: consumer, buyer, customer and clientele. The most important criterion for measuring brand density is the cohesiveness of the preconception about the brand. Brands can only provide orientation in the market if they are highly uniformly normatively charged. In short, the strong brand orders buyers to the clientele. These patterns remain stable, despite the natural fluctuation within individuals in the customer body.

The 4-K Scheme
- The *consumer* is unattached with regard to the brand performance, he is a neutral market participant: Similar to a kiosk buyer in a train station, he enters a store to realize his needs as quickly as possible. There is hardly any claim to build up a lasting customer relationship here or it would require considerable effort to explain the performance to the consumer and to make

(continued)

him a long-term "persuader". It is therefore irrelevant for brand management.

- The *buyer* has already had experience with a service and knows "that he can basically do no wrong". The brand belongs to his "relevant set", but does not necessarily have to be present. If his product is out of stock, he also reaches for the competitor's product. Conclusion: He is also not a reliable factor for the company and is unsuitable as a long-term financier.
- The *customer* regularly buys a certain product, and the same applies to the *clientele*. Both types regard the brand as an important part of their everyday life. With the customer comes the first regularity in the brand body, an initial stability characterizes the relationship of trust, the calculation security is significantly increased.
- The *clientele* is the social enhancement form of the customer; they blindly rely on the brand performance they are familiar with and are happy to recommend the brand to their circle of acquaintances. The clientele is also the experience memory of a brand. The customer is unconditionally loyal to "his" brand, but his bond is shaped by individual experiences, whereas the customer literally "believes" in a collective judgment.

This typology is a valuable approach to describe the consistency and thus future viability of a brand body. Above all, it is about quantifying the quantity ratio of the 4-Cs within the brand system. The knowledge of the proportions serves as a starting point to operationalize the stability, the degree of assertion and the future development lines of a brand.

Brands are particularly stable if they consist largely of customers. The higher the proportion of customers, the less alternative the product is. A high proportion of customers or even consumers, on the other hand, suggests a large proportion of barely networked, predominantly rationally buying individuals. Such a system is not stable, is easily irritated and has to try again and again to win people over, for example by price promotions. The effort for such campaigns and the persuasion work are immense.

Interestingly, we humans have an unmistakable sense of whether a brand is based on a stable customer base or "works" based on walk-ins and vagabond consumers. Clearly, the more sensitive a brand is to price promotions (i.e., the more frequent the use of reductions), the more insecure a brand feels about its customer body. For the green market, there is usually a high proportion of customers and clientele: The higher price level alone makes the clientele immune to attempts to poach them. For the green market, this means that the higher price is a clear signal of sophisticated refinement of the product (and allows for differentiation).

The question of which condition exists is primarily measured by the degree of networking within a group in relation to a brand. The key question is: Has networking led to the emergence of certain prejudices?

With regard to the *field of action population, the* following contents result for the questionnaire of the analysis:

Questionnaire for the Field of Action Population
- Who were the first customers?
- Are there still many customers in the start-up phase?
- How does a customer normally learn about the brand for the first time?
- Who buys the brand and how often (description of the typical customer or "buying persona")?
- Are there any events that have had a particularly positive/negative impact on the brand's reputation?
- Are there recurring statements regarding the brand among the clientele?

---

4. **Dimension: Distribution**

Distribution characterizes the path of the product/service to the customer. This area is particularly sensitive for a brand system, as external actors can have a massive influence on the style here. The importance of retail is therefore significant because the customer—with the exception of direct sales—usually does not come into contact with the retailer directly, but through an intermediary. How is the product presented in a store? Finely draped in the middle of the shelf or lying in the chute? Constantly "marked down" by red pen and discount promotions or continuously one price/range? These conditions of presentation have a fundamental impact on the customer's conceptual context. The trade thus has an immense influence on the quality of the brand appearance, since the customer does not separate between manufacturer and sales. Thus the company wooden radio was repeatedly faced with the question of whether a large department store group could sell wooden radio (in addition to the obligation to release it under competition law). From a purely economic point of view, we would have had to say "yes" without hesitation. However: The limitation already inherent in the production method (up to the waiting lists) makes clear the fact that the product cannot be sold en masse anywhere and that wooden radios are unique pieces. Especially with regard to the fact that the majority of consumer electronics today is a mass product that is replaced (i.e. thrown away) after a short time (despite being functional), the wooden radio embodies a counter-concept. Against this background, a POS that is typical for mass sales is diametrically opposed to the brand idea. Although there is an obligation to deliver, wooden radio cannot meet this obligation because too few radios are produced. This weakness turned into a strength: Starting in 2016, wooden radio communicated that new radios would start arriving in the fall of each year and that people could sign up for waiting lists. This performance context once again makes the time-intensive manufacturing process of each individual radio clear to the customer.

A strong brand succeeds, following its own understanding of values, in winning an appropriate place for itself. This place does not necessarily have to be of high quality, on the contrary: for some brands, it is precisely the "inexpensive" presentation that is decisive. If the brand is perceived by retailers as strong in its price segment and quality store, it is automatically given an appropriate place. However, if a brand shows weakness, this is perceived sensitively by the decision-makers in the retail trade and is immediately made an issue of: In most cases, the product immediately loses its traditional place. Indicators for distribution genetics are revealed by the questions formulated in the questionnaire.

With regard to the *field of action Distribution, the* following contents result for the questionnaire of the analysis:

Questionnaire on the Field of Action Distribution
- Which retail types sell the product (specialist retailers, supermarkets, hypermarkets, discounters, direct sales, Internet)?
- In which channels is how much sold?
- What is the company's sales philosophy?
- In the environment of which other brands is the product presented?
- Does the appearance follow a predefined stylistic line or does the trade dictate the style?
- To what extent has the appearance (further) developed since its foundation?
- In addition to the classic distribution analysis, a brand body should also be examined in terms of its price. The decisive factor here is above all the uniformity of the pricing of a product or service:
- How has the price stability or price range evolved over time until today?
- What role did and do special offers and discount campaigns play?

5. **Dimension: Management**

Hardly anything is more decisive for the development of a brand than the executive of brand management. Hardly anything is as decisive for the understanding of brand management as the question of who leads (e.g. family business or manager without personal connection). This system element is primarily concerned with listing the history and development of a company as well as its social or market-relevant change processes in order to place management decisions in an overarching context.

The green business sector in particular is characterised by many micro and medium-sized companies. These small companies are often characterized by "convinced" doers who want to act "differently" with their company. In connection with the work on wooden radio, we were able to meet many such company founders who, coming from the "classic economy", were inspired by the idea of interpreting their classic know-how "green". Whether it was a print shop or a fashion label, "pure, optimized money-making" was not the driver of engagement in any of the conversations. What does this mean for brand management? The forces and management that drive the green economy are characterized by the highest credibility. It is therefore all the more important to pick up on these positive motivations again and again and to link the differentiation from the classic product range with the experiences of the entrepreneurs.

Many third and fourth generation medium-sized entrepreneurs have decided in recent years to go for the "green option". Especially the price decline and the purchasing conditions in highly competitive predatory markets make the green market also economically attractive and sustainable. The Kneipp brand, founded by the Würzburg pharmacist Leonhard Oberhäußer, is characterized by its orientation towards naturopathic methods and active ingredients. The preparations are based on natural plant essences and other pure ingredients—in principle, therefore, a concrete precursor of "green products". However, the emphasis on this de facto green performance philosophy only came with the relaunch in 2005 under the guiding principle "Kneipp has been working. Since 1891". The Speick company pursues a similar strategy: founded in 1928 by entrepreneur and anthroposophist Walter Rau, the company has always pursued the idea of producing gentle, natural soaps. The basic ingredient is the Speick plant. In the following decades, the brand developed successfully, but hardly presented this natural background. It was only with the mass acceptance of the "green lifestyle" that the brand offensively used its credible green biography and nowadays trades under the name: Speick Naturkosmetik.

With regard to the *field of action management, the* following contents result for the questionnaire of the analysis:

> **Questionnaire for the Field of Action Management**
> - What is the connection between the product and the founder's biography or professional experience?
> - Which management and development principles apply in the company?
> - What are the forms of community building and company culture?
> - How is employee care practiced in concrete terms?
> - Is there a profit distribution in the company?

4.2.3 Step 3 to Strengthen Value Creation: What Exactly Describes the Success Profile of the Brand?

The actual dynamic of success of strong brands lies in the fact that collective trust can only develop if a company acts in a typical manner over a long period of time. Through the clear definition of performance, which encompasses all presences of the brand, a company is forced to act in an expectable corridor of performance and style, i.e. to remain true to itself and its unique structure. External factors or influences are not excluded, but rather integrated in a self-similar way by adapting to the success profile, or else completely discarded as "unsuitable"—not out of psychological feelings or against the background of a personal judgement of liking, but on the basis of the internal logic of the brand system. Good brand management does not know a general "right" or "wrong", but only a "this is right or wrong for *this* brand!"

The overall composition of the success components results in the "success profile of the brand". When defining a success module, it is crucial to find out whether the respective performance context that has been worked out is systemically relevant for the brand. In other words: What would happen if this success building block did not exist? Would this still be the brand that is known? Does the success module appear significantly in customer reports?

The Ovomaltine table bin from the Neuenegg manufacturer of the famous Swiss malt beverage (Wander AG) is an object that stood on almost every Swiss hotel breakfast table until the 1980s and is still remembered today. A typical accessory, for example a special bathrobe for a wellness hotel or an advertising figure such as the Michelin man, can be decisive for a brand, even if it does not directly contribute to value creation. It is played back again and again by the clientele and is thus a crystallization core of the brand.

As previously described, brands have a minimum of five and a maximum of 15 building blocks. If a brand is constituted by less than five building blocks, it is unstable and fails to build a resonant network of interacting services capable of creating a brand image. If a brand has too many building blocks for success, it cannot maintain its raison d'être, which is to reduce complexity (brand separation would be required). A brand with too many services is not manageable.

The success modules form the content-related basis for the further development, the innovation scope of the brand. The integration of further services is possible in principle, but it must be checked whether the new service is suitable to substantially strengthen the overall brand system and to deepen the Positive Prejudice. Anything else will require a disproportionately higher expenditure of energy or weaken the brand statement in the long term. It is particularly difficult when the new service defines a completely new field; in this case, the long-term effects are usually destructive. Finally, the collective prejudice patterns regarding the brand have to be dissolved or expanded—such a process only succeeds very cautiously and over long periods of time (20–30 years for strongly anchored brands). Brands have defined themselves from a certain point in time by their unique performance, they then move in a coordinate system which they can hardly change. If they change too quickly and too abruptly in terms of content, either a new brand emerges or the existing brand disintegrates: people's preconceptions are shaken and they no longer receive what they expect. Massive customer churn is the result.

Definition of the Building Blocks of Success

The following *rules of thumb* apply when determining the *building blocks of success:*

- Write down all the performance characteristics.
- Try grouping these performance characteristics for similarities. For example, "Well-trained master craftsmen" and "Every employee undergoes extensive training" are part of an overarching performance idea.

- Once all the features have been grouped, it is necessary to work out what characterises the overarching idea of performance of all the features belonging to a topic area. The task is to find a general heading for the performance characteristics that implement the module.
- If an initial definition exists, it must be weighed up whether the description actually refers to building blocks for success.

What Makes a Success Brick a Success Brick?
- The success building block has been an essential part of brand presence for a long time (mostly since inception).
- The success module contributes significantly to the value creation of the company—without it the company would run into economic difficulties (is not relevant for all success modules).
- The success module triggers a high level of resonance among customers and beyond. So far, the success module has been adapted again and again to the changing customer needs in a self-similar way.
- The effects of the success module can be directly experienced by the customers.
- The building block of success is part of the collective memory within the company and among the regular customers and is also played back by young employees or customers as a special feature.
- The success module has an outstanding position for the external effect (advertising/PR) and is remembered above average.

The Success Profile of the Wooden Radio Brand

In order to clarify the normative character of success profile and success module as well as performance, some success modules as well as the respective performance components of the brand wooden radio are described in the following The following success modules as well as the performance components behind them form the brand wooden radio:

1. **The brand name "wooden radio":** The name is a company, product and brand name and makes the field of action clear. Time-consuming explanatory work is omitted in favour of a clear anchoring of the image. The success module is realized by (excerpt):
   - Company name
   - Branding on the packaging
   - Use on documents, catalogues, trade fair stand, press releases and in telephone customer contact
2. **The wooden radio:** The original model "wr01a-2bipod" has become an eco-design icon and is internationally known through numerous media contributions. It has an above-average share of sales and is used by the media

and shops as an exposed "showpiece". The success module is realized by (excerpt):

- The original product was the wooden radio: wooden radio wr01a-2bipod
- Key visual on posters, catalogues, information brochures
- Origin of wood is part of the information for the customer
- Production process is oriented to the processing and manufacture of wood materials
- Training of the team to become wood craftsmen
- Reforestation programs are financed from the proceeds

3. **Origin Java:** The wooden radio is exclusively built, refined and packed in the home village Kandangan of the designer Singgih Susilo Kartono. From there it starts its journey into the world. The success module is realized by (excerpt):
   - The home village of the designer Kandangan, Temanggung, Central Java, Indonesia
   - Study of the designer in Bandung, Central Java, Indonesia
   - Workshop is located in the designer's home village
   - Employees are school graduates from Kandangan
   - Enclosed information brochure deals with the place of origin
   - Indication of origin in the battery compartment and on the product carton
   - Content of PR communication

4. **Detail orientated design:** wooden radios are not oriented towards design trends or supposed laws of handling. Instead, the Indonesian brand name Magno for Magnify refers to the special attention paid to sophisticated details in terms of craftsmanship. The building block of success is realized by (excerpt):
   - The New Craft concept
   - Individualized and self-developed tools and machines for design implementation
   - Sound training and quality control by the designer himself
   - Specified construction and manufacturing instructions
   - The name Magno for Magnify

5. **The craftsmen appears:** in times of anonymous mass production, wooden radios are the work of hands and people. Just as individual as the product is the origin story of the makers. They are a fundamental part of the brand understanding and appear perceptibly. The human being is not a means to an end, but an end in itself. The building block of success is realized by (excerpt):
   - Construction of the radio by a permanent team of employees
   - In some cases, the responsible employees sign the radio they made
   - Thematization and presentation of the craftsmen in articles, in the social networks and in information brochures in text and image

6. **Distribution is selective and community-oriented:** A wooden radio must not be available for purchase everywhere, but only in the appropriate places. The understanding of the distinctiveness of the brand encompasses all expressions of life—including the sales locations, which must be coherent with the human and environmental image of the overall concept. The building block of success is realized by (excerpt):

- Interested retailers must explain and present their business concept
- Obligation (Europe-wide) to enforce a uniform selling price
- Avoidance of price or discount promotions
- Dealers are personally in contact with wooden radio
- Complaints are mostly processed unchecked and within 1 day

7. **Personal customer service from Hamburg/Germany:** Despite all ethical anchoring, in the end the customer pays a high price for his radio and may expect a smooth service—especially if there are problems. The fact that the product comes from "far away" but is "organized" in the immediate vicinity provides security and thus creates confidence that help can be provided quickly in the event of a problem. The success module is realized by (excerpt):
   - Warehouse and customer service are located in Hamburg
   - Requests are handled personally by a present or known team
   - Stamp "WOODEN RADIO Tested in Hamburg, Germany by ..." (Provided with the personal signature of the tester and packer).
   - Reference to the Hamburg Site in Brochures and on the Internet

8. **Exclusive use of harmless natural materials:** wooden radio does not use product components that are harmful to people and the environment. For the construction of the products, only wood is used that comes from plantations and/or would normally be used by the local population for simpler purposes (for example as firewood). Certifications are not a must, as long as no adequate and financially feasible solutions for micro-projects are offered by the responsible organizations—in this regard, wooden radio relies on transparent communication of the material origins and invites responsible persons. The success module is realized by (excerpt):
   - Purchase of materials only in the immediate vicinity of production (ideally, each tree trunk is 'known')
   - Documentation of the origins
   - Cooperation with local environmental organisations (WWF, Greenpeace), which monitor materials policy on the ground
   - Wherever possible, wood scraps/material declared as firewood is used.
   - No chemical protective coatings, etc.
   - Topic of material origin in PR, in brochures and on the Internet

4.2.4   Step 4 to Strengthen Value Creation: Impact on Day-to-Day Operations

The brand's success profile defines the brand structure for the future. It is the system of coordinates on the basis of which a company must evaluate future challenges and—if found to be strengthening—integrate them in a self-similar way. Therefore, the creation of the success profile is not a recurring process. Once defined, the success profile shapes the company's activities. However, it makes sense to regularly compare the success profile with the day-to-day business activities of the company:

- Are the building blocks of success still being implemented?
- What deviations have crept in?
- Which consumer/product developments are relevant? In what way could they be integrated into the success profile?

In concrete terms, the following recommendations for brand practice can be made in relation to the fields of action of the brand:

Impact on Product Management and Product Development
Self-similar brand management defines the corridor in which a company develops. Through the performance-based specifications of the success profile, new products and services can be tested to determine whether they are capable of strengthening the trust memory of a brand: Do concrete and thus verifiable brand performances flow into new products? Instead of development specifications open to interpretation in the sense of a generic statement such as "high quality", a success module defines, for example, "every product of our brand lasts 20 years". A technician or engineer can now implement this specification in a verifiable manner and drive forward the work on the product with the claim in a targeted manner. The result is products that interpret the special nature of the company in a contemporary way. For this reason, a brand-sociological mnemonic is:

> Brands do not become young through young advertising, but only through young products!

In relation to the success profile of the wooden radio brand, a new product must also have the defined success components: For example, a wireless speaker was in demand, which Singgih Kartono realized and manufactured in a two-year development period—in it, all genetic specifications were again implemented.

Impact on Advertising and Marketing
Advertising, marketing and PR are considered the domain of a creative approach to the brand, especially in many larger companies. While sales is measured by its numbers, classic marketing all too often still wins with witty ideas or unexpected solutions. Nowadays, advertising is supposed to do a lot of things: it is supposed to entertain and/or hit the zeitgeist, sometimes "pick up" customers where they are, and sometimes even "educate" them. Yet advertising has only one purpose: to promote a product or service. It is supposed to ensure higher sales. The American advertiser Rosser Reeves pointed this out more than 50 years ago: "Many advertisers assume that originality and the unusual have a mysterious power. Consequently, an ad must command attention. This is a typical example of the confusion of means and ends, for if the product is worth paying money for, it is worth paying attention to." (Reeves 1963, p. 135).

The task of long-term oriented brand advertising is to permanently strengthen trust in the brand. That succeeds, by further strengthening a positive prejudice. The material for this is provided by the success profile, because this fund alone is unmistakable and defines the brand as a brand. However, this does not mean the communicative limitation to the performance as a pure fact, but rather creativity can now take place internally as well as externally in a clear corridor. The company defines the success components to be advertised, sometimes even the components/ services to be integrated, and can demand creative interpretation on this basis. The quality of an advertisement is then consequently measured by the question of whether the given content has been implemented in an appealingly creative manner. Any deviation from the content may be possible, but has the consequence that positive prejudices are not further strengthened and new content terrain must be laboriously fought for. In this sense, the success profile specifies the advertising and communication pattern and reduces the discussion effort within the company as well as for external service providers.

Impact on Market Research
Market research only makes sense if the results are considered under the focus of the success profile. The call "for cheaper prices" is obsolete for strategy development if the success profile defines that, for example, the "appropriate price" is constitutive for the brand. The task of meaningful communication is then to clarify this appropriate higher price argumentatively in the sense of a proof of performance. For example, the ecofair clothing brand "Armed Angels" advertised under the slogan "Made by humans" in the following way with a poster modelled on the H&M advertising style, on which two price quotations could be found next to a jumping model: The red crossed-out price was €39.90, the black price was €99.90. This was a reversal of the normal understanding of price in the sense of brand positioning.

> Changing consumption and buying habits must be taken into account by every brand in the sense of self-similarity. However, these changes must be perceived and then made "typical" for the brand in a controlled process.

Brand sociologists do not like to work with the term "target group", as this idea suggests that a company makes itself the recipient of certain customer wishes and adapts by targeting new customers. Strong brands are always senders and never receivers. Through uncontrolled adaptation, brands lose their brand character. Against this background, it is important to combine success profile and market research.

As soon as the success modules of the brand have been worked out, the importance, i.e. the relevance or leverage effect of the individual success modules can be measured by experienced market research. This results in a relevance ranking that allows direct forecasts regarding the communicative impact of a success module. In addition, an assignment of relevance based on various socio-demographic parameters ensures that different success modules can be used specifically in the communication of different customer groups. This form of market research is thus carried out within the framework of the brand structure and is designed in such a way that it consistently strengthens the positive bias with regard to a brand.

Impact on Distribution

Nowadays, the quality of a sales department is often measured by its reports. All too often, (supposed) competitor activities observed on the "front line" are passed on to one's own departments and the management with an urgent voice of alarm and have the tenor that the competition is "faster, more innovative and also cheaper". The quintessence is always identical: competition far ahead, we hardly exist. This unrest, carried from the outside to the inside, sometimes leads to serious consequences for the brand strategy, because it is no longer the inner compass of the company that determines the decisions, but external (supposed) signals. It is certainly important and correct to diagnose market changes, but they are never pacesetters for one's own strategy. Meaningful and long-term tactics can only emerge from the company itself, from its special know-how and its structures, which are well established in a positive sense. This is the origin of the "green corporate strategy" that is rightly postulated as reprehensible: Without taking into account the real achievements of a company that constitute the image of a brand, a new image is "flanged" onto the brand. This may be desirable and an objective of management, but it is not in fact fulfilled. It is particularly destructive to the brand when a supposed reorientation is justified ecologically, but then turns out to be an economically calculated move: Marcel E. Brenninkmeijer, investment manager of the C&A family, for example, postulated the abolition of fossil fuels in favour of regenerative energies in the interest of descendants. "The preservation of creation is a matter of course for me," Brenninkmeijer is quoted as saying. However, after the end of the solar and wind energy boom, the textile clan is getting out of numerous green projects again and investing in the lucrative extraction of oil and gas in North America. The targeted return of 15% is achievable there, while green projects rarely produced positive results in the early years. Good for the account, bad for the reputation, but only because one had previously moved into "green terrain" with high publicity.

Corporate communication often forms an advertising island that leads to irritation. In relation to green brands, however, it goes hand in hand with a breach of trust: the brand is not as it claims to be in a highly sensitive area characterised by ethics.

▶   **This Also Applies to Sales**
   Only what is inherent in the genetics of the company can be strived for. Anything else cannot establish itself in the long term and is at best capable of irritating the existing clientele.

4.3   How to Redevelop Green Brands?

The performance profile maps the future brand development from the analysis of the past. Against this background, the question arises as to how new brands or brands yet to be founded can develop assertiveness on the basis of a brand sociological analysis. In this task, the goal is to define real performance fields in advance, to build them up in a controlled manner and to implement them in day-to-day business. Instead of reading off the success profile from the past, the procedure is reversed for a young brand or a brand yet to be founded: A specific "construction plan" is worked out in advance, which defines a precise procedure for brand development.

At the start, the "images" to be achieved, i.e. effects in the clientele, are named: For example, the young brand can be used for special images for

- Naturalness
- Accessibility
- Craftsmanship

stand. The cause-effect principle of the success profile is reversed (cf. Table 4.1). As described, the previously mentioned images cannot be a guideline for a controlled brand building oriented towards the development of a Positive Prejudice. Brands only succeed in bundling collective trust under one name if they act on the cause level. Therefore, the previously mentioned image-oriented effects must now be decisively examined for their performance content. This can be achieved in a first step by means of the following guiding questions:

Guiding Questions for Brand Building
1. **Guiding questions special feature**
   - What should be special about the service? What is unique?
   - What is individually special about the idea of naturalness, accessibility and craftsmanship for the brand to be founded?
   - What should the customer/interested party associate with the product as a core service?
   - What should the brand stand for?
2. **Key questions product**
   - What does the product do?
   - Which raw materials are used?
   - Who makes it?
   - What is the exact production process?
   - Which tools/machines are used—why?
   - Are certain quality certificates etc. available?
3. **Guiding questions design**
   - Which design features should stand for the brand?
   - Are there links from history that can be transferred to the brand in terms of design?
   - What style should the brand stand for?
   - How do we implement it in terms of design?
   - What should the customer remember?

(continued)

4. **Guiding questions place**
   - Where can the brand be purchased/what distribution channels?
   - What is the ideal ambience and stylistic environment for the brand presence (on the Internet: what stylistic specifications are to be implemented)?
5. **Guiding questions employees**
   - What does the ideal salesperson/consultant for the brand look like?
   - What is he absolutely allowed to do, what is he not allowed to do?
   - How does a typical sales call go?
   - What is the decisive sales argument in direct conversation with the customer (attention: maximum three sales arguments)?
6. **Key questions customers**
   - Which customer body is the brand aiming at? Consumers or clientele (see Sect. 4.2.2).
   - What characterizes the ideal customer?
   - What should the customer spontaneously think of when the brand name is mentioned?
7. **Guiding questions resonance fields**
   - Are there learned ideas about the country/region of origin ("wine from the hillsides of the Moselle")?
   - Is there historically anchored knowledge ("This village is known for ..." or "Generations of craftsmen have ...").
   - For newcomers to the market, it makes sense to fall back on already existing, collectively stored empirical values if they are comprehensibly and authentically suited to a new product. For example, the origin "mountain cheese" will automatically evoke an idea of "purity" and "naturalness" in the reader.

Table 4.1 Cause-effect principle of the success profile

Effect/image	Cause
Naturalness	Exclusive use of eco-certified raw materials
Accessibility	Broad-based distribution
Craftsmanship	Each product is manufactured in a traditional factory

Table 4.2 Success components condition images

Building block for success	Image
Cheese is processed according to a 600 year old tradition	Originality
Each product is made from 100% organic cotton No artificial additives	Environmentally friendly Purity
The dairy farmers are introduced personally A radio is created in 16 h of manual work	Trustworthiness Genuine handwork/craftsmanship

For example, in order to refer to the special originality and exoticism of the product, the wooden radio brand primarily uses the indication "Made in Java" and rather rarely, or only where it is legally required, the description of origin "Made in Indonesia". This approach is based on the experience that "Java" automatically conjures up images of classic and untouched nature/exoticism in our mind's eye, while "Indonesia" hardly creates any images in people's minds. A brand start-up has the opportunity to integrate such "resonance fields" directly into the brand development in advance. Strategically well used origins are free resonance drivers for young brands that still have little history of their own.

Once the concrete performance characteristics of the brand are available on the basis of the guiding questions, it is necessary to bundle these characteristics thematically and to summarize them in concrete success modules. For new brands, one usually assumes about five to eight building blocks that constitute the brand and evoke the previously defined images (see Table 4.2).

The respective success modules are backed up by concrete services. It is crucial that all services to be developed are available with the success profile. They form the concrete material with which differentiation from the competition is possible—provided that these services are also clearly communicated.

An interesting example of the integration of sustainability aspects into existing, brand-compliant performance structures can be found at Coca-Cola. In its long brand history, the company has succeeded in anchoring certain positive biases worldwide. An important building block of success is that you can get a Coke everywhere (except North Korea or Cuba), i.e. the global ubiquity of the product. Whether it's at a train station kiosk or in a luxury hotel, in a desert village or in New York, you'll find a can or bottle of the fizzy drink in no time. What does this have to do with "green"? If global ubiquity is a performance characteristic of the brand, it can be used specifically for "good causes". It was against this background that the organization "ColaLife "was born. The founder and former development aid worker Simon Berry explains: "During my stays abroad I noticed that you can buy a Coke almost everywhere. But medicines for children were not. I wanted to take advantage of this sales experience of the corporation." (Novak 2012, p. 40). Now, anti-diarrhea kits for children are shipped in the Coke boxes to be delivered-sometimes urgently needed medications. A perfect solution from the point of view of brand sociology: a building block of the brand's success is used positively in a "green" sense and thus simultaneously illustrates the brand's excellent sales performance to the public.

Resonance Fields: Free Enforcement Energies on the Market
It can be observed that green brands operate in certain "imaginary worlds". It is initially irrelevant whether this is a one-man business or a "green division" within a multinational company. This is surprising because the green product and service portfolio is extremely heterogeneous. However, as was made clear in Sect. 3.3.2 "The brand from a socio-economic point of view", it is structurally completely irrelevant in the first step what the actual performance of a brand system is, as long as a group of people feels attracted to this performance. In the case of green brands, this attraction is based on specific imaginary worlds that give a product or

service a "mental home". "Green" is also integrated into fixed cultural patterns and imaginary worlds into which we as humans grow and which, in their similarity, make communication possible in the first place. The "green brand" is not a special case in the history of the brand article, because it too should or must succeed in nothing other than removing anonymity and building trust. Instead of "ignorance", people are supposed to develop ideas and expectations under a name, and in the best case a brand benefits from a clearly charged store of prejudices. The generalizing character of collective imaginaries is often criticized because it obscures the unprejudiced view towards people and groups. However, the reality of life shows that we are constantly dependent on the orienting function of prejudices. For enforcement in highly competitive displacement markets, their use is even unavoidable. For:

> The brand does not want to produce reasoned judgements, but effective pre-judgements.

In terms of brand sociology, however, it is not only geographical origins in the sense of "Made in ..." that can generate certain prejudice worlds (purity of the Alps, precision from Germany, exoticism from Bali, design sophistication from Italy), but all expressions of life of a brand. The following contexts of a brand can represent "origin":

- Historical circumstances, recalling epochs, e.g. "Woven in the tradition of Rügen beach chairs", etc.
- Genealogical roots, e.g. "family business", "owner-managed", "third generation".
- Spiritual attitudes (eco, fair-trade)

Every offer of a brand links to culturally existing ideas. By linking to an origin, the culturally existing collective ideas about this origin are quasi automatically linked to a brand. These existing cultural ideas are the so-called "resonance fields" of a brand. The brand-identifying linkage is referred to as a "resonance pattern". It describes the concrete "docking" of a brand to existing collective experience values, which sometimes reach back over several centuries, i.e. are deeply anchored in the collective consciousness of a culture. "Wine from France", for example, is considered to be of high quality, whereas "wine from Denmark", for example, has no functioning resonance field. People compose—without coercion—a connection between an individual product or service and its (ideal) origin from overarching empirical values. In this way, the anthropologically deeply rooted desire to keep the world manageable is redeemed by the resonance field-oriented brand. Brands with an origin have the valuable property of guiding people along unambiguous imaginary paths. Because origin evokes the future. With origins, products/services differentiate themselves in the market and stand for a specific performance structure in the history of experience. For the brand, the targeted integration of resonance fields means charging itself with certain ideas right from the start. Long-term brand management is therefore never about changing people's perception, but rather about achieving a certain perception (see Table 4.2).

Brand origin and resonance pattern dock with each other to activate an existing pattern, which the brand interprets sensitively, i.e. self-similarly in its sense and continues.

References

Carlson D, Richards B (2010) Time to rethink design. David Report 2010 (12/March): (keine Seitenzahlen vorhanden) (Falsterbo)

Domizlaff H (2005) Die Gewinnung des öffentlichen Vertrauens, Ein Lehrbuch der Markentechnik. Marketing Journal, Hamburg

Dunn JL (2016) Wooden radios, bamboo bicycles and human cocoons. http://dev.spedagi.org/publication2/. Zugegriffen. 29. März 2016

Kapferer JN (1992) Die Marke. Mi-Wirtschaftsbuch, München

Novak A (2012) Brause Tabletten. Interview mit Simon Berry. Enorm 01/2012. Hamburg

Papanek V (2014) Design for the real world: human ecology and social change. Thames & Hudson

Reeves R (1963) Werbung ohne Mythos. Kindler, München

Tischner U, Schmicke E, Rubik F, Prösler M (2000) Was ist EcoDesign? Ein Handbuch für ökologische und ökonomische Gestaltung. Frankfurt Main, Form-praxis

Brand Management: The Six Principles of Green Brand Management

5

Abstract

After the methodology and the use of the brand success profile have been clarified, the structure and the mode of action of the brand phenomenon have been derived and the development of the "green economy" has been illustrated, basic rules for the management of green brands can be derived. In this chapter, the "Six Laws of Green Brand Management" are summarized for use in day-to-day business. In this way, concrete parameters are available to check whether a brand tends to strengthen or discharge its brand power.

The following green branding principles apply:

- They create community through transparency.
- They confine themselves to their own performance territory.
- They communicate selected aspects of the value chain.
- They use facts, evidence of competence and explanatory examples.
- They maintain their self-similar performance and advertising pattern.
- They tie into collective patterns of resonance.

5.1 Green Brands Create Community Through Transparency

Green brands function like families: people talk openly, celebrate and argue. Everything has to be said.

Green brands are characterized by the fact that—in contrast to classic companies—their success profile is often open. People do good and talk about it a lot out of inner conviction—even if many do not yet orchestrate their actions in the sense of a perfectly marketing machine. In doing so, the speaking is not limited to the good of the performance, the product advantages, but ideally encompasses the entire value creation staircase that precedes the product presence: from the inventor/producer of the goods/service to the packaging, the development of the distribution network or the selection of the power supplier at the company headquarters. In terms of brand sociology, this is understandable: The decisive differentiating feature of green brands compared to classic companies is to understand brands not only as a means to an end. Ideally, the buyer is a co-actor in a value-creation community, *a* conscious supporter of an idea. Buyer and producer are not only benevolent towards each other in terms of service provision, the special feature of green brands is that in the ideal case the purely factual product benefit is encased in a shared idea of a "more sustainable world". The relationship is thus characterised by solidarity between producer and buyer. This leads to a permanent conflict of goals: as soon as a company demands authenticity, it de facto loses precisely this performance characteristic ...

Green brands are therefore based more on community dynamics than on social dynamics. If those responsible are aware of this, it also becomes clear why green companies must act in a particularly transparent manner: In an intact family, (almost) nothing is secret. This attitude gives rise to trust—a social cement that survives crises and, in the case of a family, functions across generations. A prerequisite for this, however, is close participation in the everyday life of the family member. Too much secrecy or even dishonesty is even more disturbing in a communal relationship than in "rough" society, to which little good is attributed anyway. The effects of this claim were made clear by the example of the green brand Hess Natur:

Example

Hess Natur, one of the first natural textile stores in Germany, was taken over by Neckermann in 2001 and eventually merged into the KarstadtQuelle Group. In 2010, the company was to be taken over by the American financial investor Carlyle Group. An affront, because Carlyle also stood for a commitment to the arms industry—and a member of the board of the Carlyle Group was George W. Bush. The authenticity of the brand was fundamentally endangered: Can a company with such a strong position still be truly "green"? A cooperative was formed by committed employees, customers and interested parties who wanted to "save" the company as a *truly* green enterprise. Finally, the company, or rather its green soul, survived when the socially committed CEO Götz Werner bought the company. ◄

These developments make it clear how sensitively and across the board the clientele perceives brand actions and demands collective honesty. "Ben & Jerry is like Amnesty International in a waffle" was a whispered description of the frozen fans of the two eco-ice pioneers Ben Cohen & Jerry Greenfield, who started selling calorie bombs for a better world in a converted petrol station in 1978. When the brand became part of the Dutch-British Unilever empire in 2000, it had sold its "soul" for many customers, although Unilever officially continues its social commitment even though it featured Collin Kaepernick.

In purely factual terms, brands are of course not in the social position of a father or a mother, and yet the analogy used earlier provides initial clues for the management of green brands: Green brands must be forthcoming about their origins and trajectories. They need to talk openly about their fortunes and misfortunes and involve the customer in the dialogue, perhaps even in the solution—without becoming unfaithful to themselves. Especially when analyzing today's digital branding demands, it becomes clear that many green brands have pioneered a new (digitally based) understanding of communication between manufacturer/provider and customer. In the past, green brands have acted more intelligently than the classic market—with the result that today they meet the attitude to life of many people and often occupy top positions in surveys of the most likeable brands.

The "paternalism" of classic marketing that presses its way into the market, as well as the ever-decreasing general acceptance of advertising—make "open" communication far more efficient. People want to be able to inform themselves and form their own judgments. This requires a "democratic understanding of information" on the part of manufacturers, who willingly enable this through transparent interaction with the clientele (so-called "instant trust").

Swiss consumer researcher David Bosshard draws attention to a new understanding of this exchange: "Only if I learn to give can I also assume that I will get something back; only if I listen will I be heard. Thus, a new economy is slowly emerging beyond conventional notions of the state and the market." (Bosshard 2011, p. 33).

This style goes even further: if you look at the interior design of green retailers, it is only consistent that mostly the impression of "cosy homeliness" is to be conveyed. Here, the brand consistently implements the "family idea" and either turns the salesroom into a "living room" or takes the customer back to the "good old days", where "good and old" means an era freed from the mania for optimisation and countless consumer insights, the driving forces of which were communal.

The Wala company also lives "green" internally: There are seven transparent salary levels in the company. Social benefits, for example a separate child allowance, decrease as soon as you move up the salary scale. A special detail: 80% of the salary is paid at the beginning of the month to cover running costs, 20% at the end of the month. The Teekampagne brand also works in a particularly catchy way: what started as a university demonstration project by Prof. Günter Faltin has become the German market leader for green and black Darjeeling tea since 1985. One of the principles: The product calculation is fully disclosed every year again.

What does this mean for "green" brand communication? In terms of brand sociological management, the success profile acts as a compass and review filter for all measures: The elaborated components form the crucial material for the targeted building and strengthening of collective trust in the brand. By first working out the real achievements of the brand in isolation and then using them in communication, the company develops from within itself. There is no need for inappropriate advertising islands, orientation towards non-brand trends or interchangeable marketing fashions. For the controlled communicative use, it is necessary to filter out the decisive proofs of performance and to use them as composition material for advertising and PR. The specific content can then be creatively edited, but it—and only it—must be integrated. By limiting itself to company-specific realities, the communication is coupled

- to the concrete performance of the company and thus has a feedback effect: "I perceive what is being done and the communication confirms it to me."
- prevents "vision marketing" that has nothing to do with the actual company (and in the worst case evokes "green washing").

5.2   Green Brands Are Limited to Their Own Performance Territory

> To be specific, the brand's success profile, its specific genetic code, must be present. Only on this basis can a brand focus and build clear bias structures.

A product becomes a brand when it succeeds in being specific. In brand-sociological logic, everything recognizable is always unique. It is not a matter of producing an original performance in all fields, but of pursuing an individual approach to a solution with regard to one or more details. An optimum is reached when as large a group of people as possible considers this new solution to be practicable and good and is prepared to pay for it. A feedback performance system has thus emerged, a natural branding has taken place.

If specialness is a basic condition for the existence of a brand, it is just as important to focus on these special contents when enforcing the brand. Such an approach prevents creative arbitrariness or interchangeability, which makes it difficult for the public to memorize the "special character of the brand". It is crucial that a brand does not make use of content that is not part of its own design territory. Too often the essence of the brand is directed towards a "consistent product or service quality". Brand work begins when every special feature of the daily business, no matter how small, is researched and defined and is available as a "treasure trove of the company" for targeted selection and continuous use.

It is always important to analyze the overall system of the brand: The product or the service is only one expression of the brand's life, although it is undoubtedly the most important one. But analytically just as important are all areas that the customers can perceive: Every brand is always an overall composition of various highly individual elements. In the case of the wooden radio brand, for example, the high quality of workmanship was undoubtedly of extraordinary importance for its entry into the European market and remains the basis of its business to this day. In order to make the qualitative value and uniqueness of the radio concrete for the clientele, the product-technically irrelevant, but for this perception of the radio important imprint is decisive, which was placed in the battery inner housing and shows a handwritten manufacturing number.

Brand design expressions, which may not be directly related to product quality, are sometimes part of the overall concept of a brand. A well-groomed flight attendant has no effect on the technical condition of the aircraft. However, an unshaven flight attendant wearing a stained jacket would raise doubts among passengers about the perception of the airline as safe.

5.3   Green Brands Communicate Selected Aspects of the Value Chain

A green brand must remain self-similar to its advertising pattern.

Advertising and communication function homologously to all other steps of the value creation staircase of a brand. Marketing has the sole task of disseminating the previously performed refinement steps of a brand in a resonant way (it is irrelevant whether one wants to communicate a classic product or a service).

The top advertising task is to translate the technical or service-oriented benefits in a way that resonates and thus has mass appeal, and to find communicative levers to anchor this individual content in a memorable way. Under the motto "One-for-One", the green shoe brand TOMS donates another pair of shoes to a person in need for every pair sold.

Another positive example is the Hamburg-based company lemonaid.

Example

One of the core values of the lemonaid company is to treat people and nature fairly. An outstanding lemonaid communication solution works like this: To make it concrete that a person should be treated decently—and regardless of where they live—the creators dreamed up deposit collection boxes. They had noticed that homeless people in the hip party districts of the metropolises were searching for deposit bottles with their bare hands in dirty trash cans, while the young party people were partying carefree (and emptying plenty of bottles in the process). The company's founders devised a way to prepare the deposit boxes so that they could be placed underneath trash cans and labeled them, "Help deposit collectors! Going through trash cans is dangerous—and humiliating. So put your deposit bottles next to it. Or in this box. Thank you." The action was subsequently spread on social media networks and met with a great response. With this "good" idea, a brand succeeds in communicating its philanthropic anchoring in a smart and interesting way—this, too, is only possible if the brand's own building blocks for success have been defined beforehand. ◄

The Berlin Bio Company or also the Münsterland dairy Söbbeke advertise with their own employees or associated farmers, although the company has been producing and processing milk for more than 120 years, but has only been operating "organically" for 20 years—also in order to escape the consolidation processes and price wars in the conventional dairy industry. The specific glass added value concept from 1989 quickly became a differentiating feature of the company. In 1998, they were one of the first companies to sell yoghurts without additional flavourings (until then this had been considered impossible).

5.4   Green Brands Use Facts, Evidence of Competence and Explanatory Examples

People construct abstract judgments from concrete facts—never the other way around.

Many well-intentioned assertion strategies fail to be skilfully implemented in the market. Numerous people are so brazen and simply do not react to the carefully conceived (advertising) message. Supposed way out: even more advertising pressure. Many advertisements work on the "image level" and lose themselves in abstract emotional worlds and dubious emotionalization strategies. The difficulty of enforcing image campaigns has been dealt with several times. From the point of view of brand sociology, advertising can only assert itself if brand-specific performance is presented in a catchy way—with facts or proof of performance. In this sense, brand-sociologically oriented advertising makes use of typical dynamics of prejudice formation: People construct universal insights from individual experiences. A good example is provided by the ERGO Insurance Group.

Example

In the highly complex insurance industry, ERGO differentiates itself through a dedicated illustration of "green" projects on its website, far beyond a classic sustainability report: project presentations, interviews and activity reports make the company tangible—right down to a personalised advertisement. Here, the brand succeeds in literally "showing its face" in the increasingly anonymous digital insurance markets. Especially in an area that requires pre-confidence (you only notice whether an insurance policy is effective afterwards), it is important to embody accessibility in an exemplary, condensed way via a "real person" and not via a distant organisation. ◄

The integration of these prejudice dynamics into every communicative utterance of the company is the challenge for marketing. Brand sociology uses existing thought patterns for this purpose, which the individual message recipient uses uncontrollably for the intended conclusions. A concretely applied communication strategy is not only based on the performance fact itself, but embeds it in collective thinking rules and experiences, judgment schemes, generally valid opinions and prejudices.

5.5   Green Brands Maintain Their Self-Similar Performance and Advertising Pattern

Self-similarity is the success principle of all living systems.

The 90-year-old Swiss brand Held is known for ecological washing and cleaning products. The brand founder Gottfried Held was a pioneer in this field. Today, the company by no means offers the identical products from the brand launch in 1923. Since that time, formulations have been constantly optimized, and the brand's packaging and appearance have adapted to the state of research and the aesthetic spirit of the times. Held has not been advertising with the identical advertising motif for nine decades, and yet today the brand stands for a certain form of service provision and public presence throughout Switzerland. Corporate practice shows that strong brands act in a self-similar manner, i.e. they ensure the retention and variation of specific performance and design characteristics over time. Especially in the case of smaller brands, this often happens intuitively, because brand sociology follows common sense—and this is extremely well developed in many entrepreneurs.

Certain forms of advertising can even become constituent building blocks of a brand's success themselves, provided that the advertising activities become conditional for public perception. For example, Johannes Gutmann, founder and head of Sonnentor Kräuterhandels GmbH, almost always appears in public wearing red glasses, the Sonnentor logo T-shirt and 80-year-old leather trousers. He has become a living trademark himself and received the Brand Ambassador Award at the Brand Life Awards in 2017.

The use of self-similar advertising patterns reduces the content-related as well as monetary effort required to anchor a message, because only subtle, "learned" impulses are needed to evoke—in the best sense—entrenched ideas and expectations in the customer. In times when attention is a valuable commodity, this form of brand development proves to be particularly assertive.

In order to make special features known, a long-lasting and clear message is needed. Therefore, today already popular brands are preferably bought up instead of creating new ones. In the best case, the already existing positive prejudices are confirmed again and again in advertising. The self-similarity of advertising takes place in a clear sequence: the success pattern of the brand provides the content for the communication and/or advertising code of the brand, it forms the creative corridor for all advertising activities.

5.6   Green Brands Tie in with Collective Resonance Patterns

Resonance patterns are content bridgeheads that automatically endow a brand with learned cultural experiential values.

Hardly any methodology is as assertive and quickly implementable as the integration and linking with collective resonance patterns. Brands are cultural bodies that themselves evoke certain ideas and expectations. There are no products or services that operate in a contextless space. On the contrary, as soon as a product is recognizable as a product, people will try to "classify" it: Where did it come from? Who produced it? What is its history? There are no products that do not (want to) evoke ideas. Even a classic "white" trade mark evokes certain ideas and expectations through its sheer design. And be it only: Cheap! Freely adapted from the scientific and literary all-rounder Paul Watzlawick: A product cannot not communicate.

People compose certain images from certain origins, which usually do not feed their contents from individual experiences, but are collective worlds of imagination that the individual person adopts. Brand-oriented communication is always related to a resonance pattern (see Sect. 4.3). With the collective resonance patterns that exist everywhere, brands have free linking energies at their disposal. Especially green products—and those that want to profit from a supposed green wave—work with numerous socially enforced elements that are supposed to convey naturalness "at first glance".

Example

The name Landliebe and a naively opulent graphic design evoke that the product seems like the epitome of a "green product". In 1987, Landliebe was the first brand to offer milk in the sustainable returnable bottle. This was a national breakthrough for the company, "aided" by the Chernobyl nuclear disaster that same year, which resulted in a run on milk protected in the jar. From 1992 onwards, yoghurt was also available in returnable jars.

Of course, the brand also follows several sustainable initiatives. In 2008, for example, it announced that Landliebe products would be produced without genetically modified plants in animal feed in the future. And yet it is (also) a clever marketing staging by the group. The background is clear: the attributes "Landliebe" and "naive design" are used to activate resonance fields that specifically give customers the feeling that they have bought a "green product". This is certainly just as possible through intensive information and advertising work, but the result would only be visible after a much longer period of time. ◄

Resonance fields do not arise ad hoc, they are the result of cross-generational experience values that can be orchestrated for a brand because they form learned emotional anchor points in a highly complex and confusing world.

Reference

Bosshard D (2011) The age of less. Murmann Verlag, Hamburg

Appendix: Conclusion and Outlook—Brand Instead of Capitalism

In a commercialized world, many green companies are a comforting exception: Often, these actors are not guided exclusively by profit or value-creation interests and place people and their environment at the center of their economic activity out of conviction. This makes it all the more difficult when elements flow into this context that, in the common understanding, belong to a diametrically opposed sense and sphere: Brand, marketing and brand advertising in their different variations, which serve the purpose of inspiring people for things they may not even need—for simple profit maximization.

Against this background, the widespread critical attitude towards such "marketing activities" is understandable. However, only insofar as the actual task of a savvy advertising activity as a communication offer is not illuminated. Only when it is clear that people have always grouped themselves around special services does it become apparent that even "green offers"—if they want to reach as many interested people as possible and thus form an antithesis to the classical economy—are subject to clear communicative rules and limitations.

However, this is only possible if brand communities are not understood exclusively as economic but also as social actors. Based on brand sociology, it was explained what characterizes a brand community and which social dynamics it is subject to. When does it reach a particularly large number of people who are sympathetic to it, and when does it generate irritation and rejection? The laws of action for successful communication are universal—regardless of whether we are talking about an organic farm, a social institution or an ecologically mindful printing company. Brand sociology borrows its scientific basis from the knowledge of the constant behavioural patterns of individual people, but above all of human interaction. Social laws that are just as valid in the age of social media and networks as they were hundreds of years ago. The tools change, the operators structurally do not.

Especially against the backdrop of the new diverse technical offers and possibilities, which are also constantly changing and determine individual behavior on the Internet, but also in the real world, it is imperative to first work out and define the "genetic code" of the individual service offer in order to act uniquely and particularly. Only in this way is it at all possible to assert one's own specificity independently of new or old communication channels and media.

© Springer Fachmedien Wiesbaden GmbH, part of Springer Nature 2022
O. Errichiello, A. Zschiesche, *Green Branding*,
https://doi.org/10.1007/978-3-658-36060-3

Green branding is a fulfilling task because green brands sell their morals on ethical terms. What does that mean? It means that every brand pushes its form of interpretation of the world, whether it's using a spread with special ingredients from an equally special farm or developing a fuel-efficient engine. The corporate desire to enrich the world through a specific service or product, to solve problems, to liberate needs, is deeply moral. Morality is always the commitment of a group. Ethics is the conception of a world in which we meet not as competitors or adversaries, but first as equal human beings who have basically the identical desires for themselves and all those close to them—and the ethical right to do so. Ethics knows no enemy, it knows only reason. That is why here one agrees on treaties, not on wars.

A green product is always a performance that specifically interprets the world at a modest point and links it to clear ethical ideas, namely the claim to treat people and our environment in such a way that we always recognize ourselves in the other. And we need this, at least if one considers the generally enforced unrestrained orientation towards the economic megalomania of "more and more". With green brands, there is the possibility of including reason parameters with a long-term economically healthy perspective—the original idea of the brand article—once again in the economic cycles. Green brands are often companies that have not yet exchanged the idea of performance for the idea of an attention-grabbing appearance.

Meeting expectations and a sharpened sensibility for people and the environment are components of ethics. Ethics is not just a pretty topic for committed speeches and lip service in time for the company's anniversary. On the contrary: ethics emerge in the day-to-day actions of the company. Brands sell ethics under moral conditions. Or: Brand instead of capitalism.

Are environmentally and socially engaged people allowed to engage with brands and brand building? They must. Because only knowledge of the brand's seemingly "unethical impact" and its inescapable collective pull as a cultural phenomenon allows green businesses and their decision-makers at all levels to make the world around them a little better. Compassion and actionism are not a viable business concept and do not permanently help the desire for a more just and responsible world. The delusion and unfortunately existing reality of global profit maximization can only be replaced by the exemplary functioning of a sustainable economy. Basically speaking:

Ideas can only be fought with ideas.

Green consumerism is often characterised by the need for simplicity, for making everyday purchases, everyday things, precious again. The everyday product becomes an expression of mindfulness and craftsmanship. In an age of automation and mass production, which allow little or no trace of origin, "the green brand" embodies history and stories: It stands for authenticity in a world in which many long for truthfulness and thereby inspires social trust. In its ideal form, the green brand realizes a world that is again small, manageable and controllable. It conveys to us that we are not target groups, but people. An extremely desirable idea.

Trust is often used as a buzzword these days. It is wonderfully diffuse and therefore allows universal use. However, if one takes trust-building seriously, trust is based solely on promise reliability: a company acts in such a way that the expected service will also be provided in the future. As a mutually supportive action, this form of exchange—as the founder of German sociology called it—is affirmative and thus social. Accordingly, trust only arises when a company acts in a normatively reliable and not "somehow good or friendly" manner.

If you want trust, you have to act.

The green brand demands a clear commitment and includes an equally clear task for those responsible for the brand: To produce things that are not facades, but are based on honest performance, have substance.

The work on this book has also revealed the balancing act between the desire to secure the livelihoods of people and, on the other hand, to strengthen the economic value creation power of companies. Our perception of this conflict of goals may indicate that thinking in terms of both spheres seems to be far from normal. The "green economy" is extremely young compared to economic history, and therefore it will still take time for a real cultural change to take place—perhaps the epoch of acceleration may also be a blessing in this context. Fundamental changes in lifestyle habits have long since ceased to be voluntary appeals, since—ecologically speaking—the time for the urgently needed "reversal" has already passed. Our generation has still not grasped the real gravity of the situation.

It is therefore not only a matter of recognizing and improving the small systemic issues in the sense of a private concern, but also of understanding ecological destruction as a universal context of an economic concept based on growth. It is also clear, however, that the new, modern companies make use of a psychological trick throughout: If in the "old economy" the legitimate purpose of a company was to make money with its products (from which everyone profited in varying degrees), today the avant-garde of the globalized economy inscribes the "improvement of the world" on its imaginary banners—if one reads the self-descriptions and mission statements of companies such as Alphabet, Amazon, Tesla, Airbnb or Ebay. But this supposed ethical stance obscures the fact that the economic conceptions of these companies at the lowest levels of the value chain are based on doing away with achievements of the pre-digital era: Everyone of us knows that Amazon doesn't pay its warehouse workers properly, everyone knows that Apple devices are manufactured under dubious conditions in Chinese factories, and everyone is aware that Google provides fruit plates for its employees and organizes adventurous company outings, but that a regular private life is not possible (that's why largely unattached twenty-somethings work there). In the area of food and luxury foods, we rely on an almost unbroken "ethical chain of good conscience" of certifications and environmental tests, and seriously consider whether the CO_2 emissions from buying an apple from non-regional production are justifiable, but in the area of technical-electronic products, this consumer culture almost completely fades into the background.

Sociologist Harald Welzer holds the following view: "Almost everything you find in your wardrobe, in your fridge, in your car, house or holiday hotel, what you communicate with, what you eat and drink, comes about in ways you do not want to know. More precisely, it comes to you at prices you don't want to know how it is possible" (Welzer 2016, p. 78). You sell products and services that themselves claim to "advance the world," to "be clean," and act inwardly structurally as they did at the beginning of industrialization. This is of little concern to us, because we are not aware of the consequences of our (purchasing) decisions in "Fortress Europe": Thousands of kilometres away in the hinterland of China, Vietnam or Indonesia stand the factories whose existence only becomes visible (briefly in the media) when they collapse or burn down. In the never-ending chain of news updates, however, these news items remain mere highlights of an already hyper-consumerist world that no longer seems to know any pauses for attention. Rapidly successive product cycles (without really essential new inventions) and electronic aids of all kinds, sizes and resolutions, which determine, consume and monitor us from the bedside table to the bus stop to the concert visit, catapult the alienation of the ego mercilessly forward. This, coupled with an almost naïve belief that the world and the relations of justice do not have to change fundamentally, but that we can continue as before—only green. This idea is not only unrealistic, but dangerous, because it transfers the level of action to the responsibility of the individual, who either treats the world with care or not, either by buying organic meat or eggs from caged hens. But the level of action is structural: an economic system based on growth cannot preserve the environment, people and animals.

Scientists point out that it is probably only ecological collapse that can lead to a profound reconstruction of sociality. The message is that simply switching from conventional to green will not change our problematic consumption patterns: The bio-fair latte machiato in the porcelain cup you bring home and then drink in the SUV is not a model for the future. The example makes it clear that the questions of "green brand management" are the very first steps on a very long path.

If entrepreneurs and scientists of the future ever bother to research the development of green consumer culture, much of it will probably strike them as very trying and inconsistent. Polite would be a shake of the head, more likely sheer horror. It will probably seem equally puzzling to them how, in the face of the challenges and the palpable devastation to people and nature, it was not possible to agree on sweeping action. Even our generation finds it difficult to comprehend, since we consider ourselves wiser, more enlightened, more sensitive and more rational than all our predecessors on this planet. All the information is available statistically.

And yet (with a view to understanding on the part of the reader of the future): The fact that this—still far too little used—green lane exists at all is thanks to those who even then sensed the connections and were prepared to seek and take risks for a "somehow better" ...

Reference

Welzer H (2016) Die smarte Diktatur - Der Angriff auf unsere Freiheit. Fischer Verlag, Frankfurt

Index

© Springer Fachmedien Wiesbaden GmbH, part of Springer Nature 2022   145
O. Errichiello, A. Zschiesche, *Green Branding*,
https://doi.org/10.1007/978-3-658-36060-3